STECK-VAUGHN

STECK-VAUGHN

Steps to Achieve

READING

Teacher's Guide

GRADE 5

Steck Vaughn™

A Harcourt Achieve Imprint

www.Steck-Vaughn.com
1-800-531-5015

Contents

Steps to Achieve

Help your English language learners and struggling readers perform at grade level and succeed on standardized tests.

Grade-level Performance!

STEP UP TO

SUCCESS

Shows students strategies for tackling grade-level skills and breaking down grade-level texts.

STEP UP TO

VOCABULARY

Reviews and supports vocabulary related to each skill.

STEP UP TO THE

BASICS

Provides a solid foundation in the skill or concept.

Reading Level 5

Reading Level 4

Reading Level 3

Grade 5 Skill

Steps to Achieve reinforces key concepts by having students complete 20 skills three times in one book.

STEP 1 — STEP UP TO THE **BASICS**
Students complete **Skill 1** through **Skill 20**.

- Skill defined
- Direct instruction of skills
- Graphic tools to aid in understanding skill
- Skill practice at grade 3 reading level

STEP 2 — STEP UP TO **VOCABULARY**
Students complete **Skill 1** through **Skill 20**.

- Skill signal words introduced
- Skill review
- Graphic tool review
- Skill practice at grade 4 reading level

STEP 3 — STEP UP TO **SUCCESS**
Students complete **Skill 1** through **Skill 20**.

- Test-taking strategies introduced
- Skill review
- Signal words review
- Graphic tool review
- Skill practice at grade 5 reading level

Students cover these 20 grade-level skills at each step in the Grade 5 book.

1. Main idea and supporting details
2. Sequence
3. Compare and contrast
4. Cause and effect
5. Character
6. Plot and setting
7. Theme
8. Literary elements
9. Structural elements
10. Visual information
11. Nonfiction writing
12. Root words, prefixes, and suffixes
13. Synonyms and antonyms
14. Context clues
15. Multiple-meaning words
16. Author's purpose
17. Facts and opinions
18. Draw conclusions and make inferences
19. Make predictions
20. Summarize

Components Overview

Student Books and *Teacher's Guides* are packed with features to ensure your students' success.

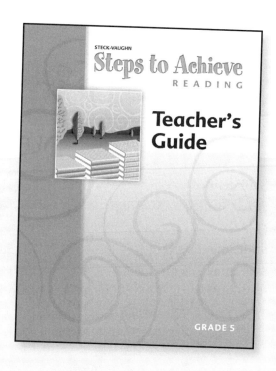

Grade 5 Student Book

- Instruction in 20 curriculum-based grade 5 skills

- Content that becomes more challenging as the student progresses through the steps

- Step-by-step guided instruction

- Small group and partner activities that encourage independent practice

- Tools, vocabulary strategies, and techniques to help students break down texts

- Ongoing opportunities for review and assessment

Grade 5 Teacher's Guide

- Detailed step-by-step directions for guiding students through each skill lesson

- Answers and Explanations for the Unit and Step Review questions

- Tracking charts to monitor student progress

- Reteaching activities to help students who need additional instruction

Instructional Plan

Each lesson has four consistent parts for an easy-to-implement instructional plan.

Learn the Skill ▷ **Apply the Skill** ▷ **With a Partner** ▷ **On Your Own**

Two flexible pacing options meet your classroom needs.

Option 1

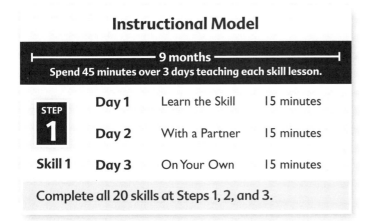

Instructional Model

9 months		
Spend 45 minutes over 3 days teaching each skill lesson.		
STEP 1 **Day 1**	Learn the Skill	15 minutes
Day 2	With a Partner	15 minutes
Skill 1 **Day 3**	On Your Own	15 minutes
Complete all 20 skills at Steps 1, 2, and 3.		

Supplement your curriculum in as little as 15 minutes a day!

Option 2

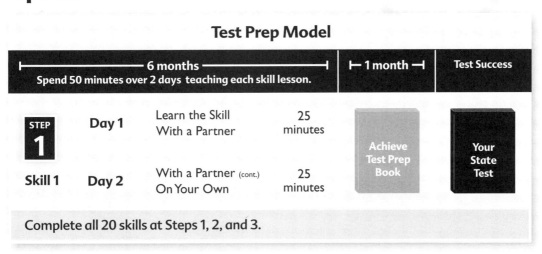

Test Prep Model

6 months		⊢ 1 month ⊣	Test Success
Spend 50 minutes over 2 days teaching each skill lesson.			
STEP 1 **Day 1**	Learn the Skill With a Partner	25 minutes	**Achieve Test Prep Book**	**Your State Test**
Skill 1 **Day 2**	With a Partner (cont.) On Your Own	25 minutes		
Complete all 20 skills at Steps 1, 2, and 3.			

Ask your Steck-Vaughn sales representative about correlations between Steps to Achieve and your state standards and about the Achieve line of state-specific test prep books.

Student Books

Cover all three steps in one book.

STEP 1

Grade 5 skill instruction at Grade 3 reading level

Presents a skill in clear, easy-to-follow steps.

Guides students in using the skill.

Provides students with tools and graphic organizers to help them master the skill.

STEP 2

Grade 5 skill review and practice at Grade 4 reading level

Refreshes students' knowledge of the skill.

Introduces signal words and other language students need to master the skill.

Encourages students to practice identifying key vocabulary words.

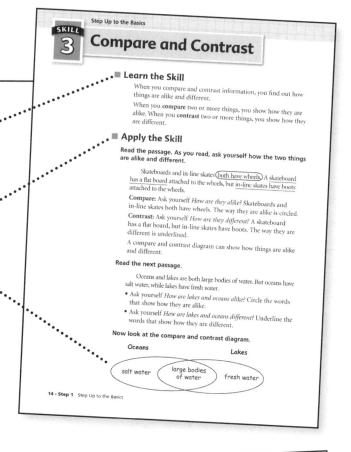

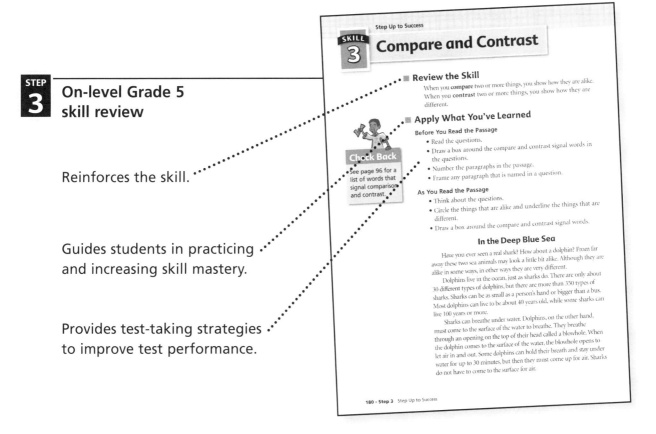

STEP 3 On-level Grade 5 skill review

Reinforces the skill.

Guides students in practicing and increasing skill mastery.

Provides test-taking strategies to improve test performance.

Step Up to Success

SKILL 3 Compare and Contrast

■ **Review the Skill**

When you **compare** two or more things, you show how they are alike. When you **contrast** two or more things, you show how they are different.

■ **Apply What You've Learned**

Before You Read the Passage
• Read the questions.
• Draw a box around the compare and contrast signal words in the questions.
• Number the paragraphs in the passage.
• Frame any paragraph that is named in a question.

As You Read the Passage
• Think about the questions.
• Circle the things that are alike and underline the things that are different.
• Draw a box around the compare and contrast signal words.

Check Back
See page 96 for a list of words that signal comparison and contrast.

In the Deep Blue Sea

Have you ever seen a real shark? How about a dolphin? From far away these two sea animals may look a little bit alike. Although they are alike in some ways, in other ways they are very different.

Dolphins live in the ocean, just as sharks do. There are only about 30 different types of dolphins, but there are more than 350 types of sharks. Sharks can be as small as a person's hand or bigger than a bus. Most dolphins can live to be about 40 years old, while some sharks can live 100 years or more.

Sharks can breathe under water. Dolphins, on the other hand, must come to the surface of the water to breathe. They breathe through an opening on the top of their head called a blowhole. When the dolphin comes to the surface of the water, the blowhole opens to let air in and out. Some dolphins can hold their breath and stay under water for up to 30 minutes, but then they must come up for air. Sharks do not have to come to the surface for air.

180 • Step 3   Step Up to Success

Research Base

Scaffolding

"*Struggling readers need access to grade-level material through a variety of scaffolded experiences (i.e. partner reading, guided reading, read-alouds) so that they are exposed to grade-level ideas, text structures, and vocabulary (Cunningham and Allington, 1999).*"

–Sheila Valencia and Marsha Riddle Buly

The Language of Testing

"*Data demonstrate that the presence of unknown vocabulary in the questions and answer choices was the major linguistic factor that adversely affected the Hispanic children's reading performance.*"

–National Research Council

Differentiated Instruction

"*Differentiated instruction is first and foremost good instruction. Many current understandings about learning provide strong support for classrooms that recognize, honor, and cultivate individuality.*"

–C.A. Tomlinson

Teacher's Guide

Clear lesson structure provides everything
you need to deliver effective instruction.

Start each lesson with clearly
stated learning objectives.

Motivate your students to identify
with the content by calling on prior
knowledge.

Use these quick pointers to
provide your students with
additional learning strategies.

Follow the step-by-step instructions to
guide your students through class, small
group, and independent activities.

Reinforce the tools, vocabulary,
and strategies students learn
with each skill.

Tailor instruction to meet the
needs of the diverse students in
your classroom.

Encourage students to write their own
definitions of key skill vocabulary.

Step 1 | Skill 3 ▪ Compare and Contrast

Objective
To use compare and contrast relationships to understand texts. Using a variety of tools, students will learn to compare and contrast people or objects in a passage, and to answer questions about compare and contrast.

Build Background
Place a tennis ball and a golf ball on your desk. Write *Compare* on the board. Ask *How are these two things alike?* Write answers such as *They are both balls; they are both round, they are both used in games.* Write *Contrast* on the board. Ask *How are these two things different?* Write answers such as *They are different colors, materials, and sizes; one is hit with a club, while the other is hit with a racket.* Tell students that when they compare two or more things, they find ways in which they are alike. When they contrast two or more things, they find ways in which they are different.

Student page 14 ▶ Learn the Skill
Discuss with students the difference between compare and contrast to be sure they understand it.

Coaching Tip
Point out to students that there may not always be an equal number of similarities and differences between two or more things.

Apply the Skill
Knowing how to compare and contrast will help students understand what they read. In this section, students will learn and use tools to help them identify and answer questions about compare and contrast.

- Write on the board *Skateboards and in-line skates both have wheels. A skateboard has a flat board attached to the wheels, but in-line skates have boots attached to the wheels.*
- Ask *How are skateboards and in-line skates alike?* (Both have wheels.) Circle the words that show how they are alike. Say *I circled the way they are similar.*
- Ask *How are they different?* (A skateboard has a flat board, but in-line skates have boots.) Underline the words that show how they are different. Say *I underlined the ways they are different.*
- Have students cover up the chart in the book as they read the next passage and circle the similarities and underline the differences. Draw an empty compare and contrast diagram on the board.
- Ask a volunteer to tell what she circled and to explain her thinking. Redirect as necessary. Record the answer in the diagram. Repeat the procedure for contrast.
- Have students compare your diagram to the one in the book to see if they match. Tell them that the compare and contrast diagram is a way to organize compare and contrast. Also tell them that they can use a diagram to help them answer questions about compare and contrast.

Student page 15 ▶ With a Partner
Have students work together and discuss their thinking with each other and with the class.

Answers
Apples
1. red, green, or yellow
2. don't have to peel
3. Vitamin A
Oranges
1. orange
2. have to peel
3. Vitamin C
Both
1. types of fruit, grow on trees
2. taste sweet
3. good for you

- Have pairs of students read the passage. Tell them not to fill in the diagram in their books yet.
- Come back together as a class.
- Say *I found one way in which apples and oranges are alike. They are a type of fruit. Did you find it?* Circle the words. *I also found a way they are different. Apples can be red, green, or yellow, but ripe oranges are always orange. Do you see it?* Underline it.
- Draw a compare and contrast diagram on the board, fill it in, and have students copy the words in the diagram in their books.
- Have students find other examples of compare and contrast relationships in the passage. Remind them to circle the ways the things are alike and underline the ways they are different. Then have them add their answers to the diagram in their books.
- Invite students to tell what they wrote in their diagrams and to explain their thinking. Redirect as necessary. Record the answers in the diagram on the board. Continue until all students have recorded all compare and contrast relationships.

8 ▪ Step 1 Skill 3 Compare and Contrast

Student page 16 ▶ On Your Own
Ask students to work independently on a short practice test.
- Encourage students to circle and underline in the passage and to draw a compare and contrast diagram.
- Come back together as a class and ask students to explain their answer choices. Redirect as necessary.

Think About
Have students review the tools they've learned before beginning the On Your Own activity.

Answers
1. C
2. A
3. B

Differentiated Instruction

English Language Learners
Bring in pictures from sports magazines that illustrate different comparisons and contrasts from this passage. Examples would include pictures of a football and soccer ball, a soccer player kicking a goal, a receiver catching a pass, and others. Read the passage again with students and show the pictures to reinforce the comparison or contrast between sports.

Struggling Learners
Invite students to compare and contrast something in their own life, such as shirts they have at home, two dogs they saw at the park, or two games they like to play. Have students take turns doing this.

Visual Learners
Write several questions on the board for students to answer on a sheet of paper. Questions might include the following: *Where do you go to school? Where do you live? What hobbies do you have? What sports do you like? How many brothers and sisters do you have? What is your favorite color?* Have students work in pairs to share their answers. Then, on a large piece of paper, have the pairs of students draw a compare and contrast diagram. Ask each student to write his or her name in one of the circles. Have them write *Both* as a heading for the overlapping area. Tell students to write what they have in common in the overlapping circle and the other information under their own name. Ask students to display their diagrams to the class.

Your Dictionary
Have students turn to page 252 and write or copy the definitions for *compare* and *contrast* and give examples. (compare—to show how two or more things are alike; contrast—to show how two or more things are different)

Step 1 Skill 3 Compare and Contrast ▪ 9

Before You Begin

Step 1 is the first step in the three-step approach and covers pages 3–84 in the student book. Instruction is at a basic level to ensure students have a solid foundation in the skills.

To meet the needs of struggling learners and English language learners, the readability is approximately two grades below level, passages are short (less than half a page), and reading material is high interest. This helps students develop fluency by allowing them to focus on the skill being taught with little distraction from the language. Beginning the book with passages that students can read independently or with little assistance will help them avoid frustration and achieve success quickly, making them feel good about what they can do on their own.

Step 1 presents reading strategies at the most foundational level, graphic organizers that are uncomplicated, and short practice passages that help students practice the skill. This attention to the basics will help students become successful and more confident readers. Use the Student Skill Progress Chart on pages 116–117 to track each student's progress on the skills. The Skills and Items Correlation on page 118 will help you identify which questions in the unit and step reviews test each skill.

Introduction to Step 1

The Introduction to Step 1 focuses on key words, tools, and text features students will use throughout the step. Ensuring that students are comfortable with these concepts before they begin skill instruction on page 8 in the student book will allow them to focus on understanding the skills. Tell students that they will learn tools that will help them manage the information they read and become better readers.

Student page 4 ▶ ## About Words to Know

Students will learn the names of parts of passages such as *paragraph* and *title*. Explain to students that these words are important because directions and questions often refer to them. For example, directions may instruct students to *Read the passage,* and a question may begin with *In paragraph 2…* or *According to the title….*

Words to Know
directions
passage
title
paragraph
question
answer choices

- Ask a volunteer to read the definition of the first word in the list (*directions*). Then give a real-life example. Say *Directions tell you what to do and how to do it. Yesterday I followed the directions for making a cake. The directions said to mix together the ingredients, pour the mix into a pan, and bake it in the oven. Did you read directions or did anyone give you directions yesterday?*
- Continue with each boldfaced word.
- Have pairs of students write the name of each part on the lines beside "A Surprise." (*title, paragraph, passage, question, answer choices*)
- Regroup as a class and have students share their answers. Redirect as necessary.
- If time permits, have students read "A Surprise" and answer the question. (1. A)

Student pages 4–5 ▶ ## About Tools to Use

Students will learn tools to help them manage and organize information in reading passages and questions. Introduce students to the concept of tools.

- Say *A hammer is a tool. What do we use it for?* (to build things) *What kinds of tools does a cook use?* (possible answers: mixer, can opener, knife, pots and pans) *What kinds of tools do you use in school or at home, and how do they help you?* (possible answers: scissors, pencil, computer, bike lock) *You can use tools when you read, too.*

Tools to Use

Underline and Circle—Students underline and circle to sort information as they read.

- Direct students to the example sentences. Ask *Which word is underlined?* (*soccer*) *Which word is circled?* (*dog*)
- Have pairs of students read the passage and underline the names of colors (*yellow, yellow, green*) and circle the words that begin with the letter *s* (*secret, Suddenly, slime, slime, said, she, she, space*).

Charts and Webs—Students use graphic organizers to organize information as they read.

- Draw a chart and a web on the board. Point out to students that charts and webs have different features.
- Say *These are two kinds of graphic organizers that you may already know about. What are they?* (a chart and a web)
- Ask students for situations when they've seen or used a chart or a web.
- Direct students to the chart on page 5 and have them fill it in. (possible answers: *plums, lemons, beans, potatoes*)
- Direct students to the web on page 6 and have them fill it in. (possible answers: *English, math, history*)

Student page 6 ▶ ## About the Think About Box

The Think About feature is one of three that students will become familiar with throughout the book. It reminds students of tools they've already learned and can apply to their reading. The Think About box appears in Steps 1 and 2.

Think About Box

- Direct students to the Think About box and explain that it lists tools they've learned. Tell them that they should review the list before they answer questions about a passage.
- Have students read the Think About box next to the short passage about Pete's birthday. Then have them read the passage and underline the names of people (*Pete, Sal*) and circle the words that were written on the sign (*Happy Birthday Pete!*).

Student page 6 ▶ ## About Your Dictionary

The Your Dictionary feature is found on pages 252–254 of the student book. As your students proceed through the 20 skill lessons in Step 1, they will write or copy definitions of key words from the lessons in their dictionary. This feature reinforces key vocabulary as well as giving students a personal resource.

Your Dictionary

- Direct students to pages 252–254 in their book. Say *This is your dictionary. It is your place to write your own definitions or copy definitions of words you will learn in this book. Writing the definitions will help you learn the words and remember what they mean.*
- Redirect students to page 6.
- Have them write the definitions in their own words or copy them from page 4. (passage—a story about something make-believe or something real; title—the name of a passage)

Unit 1: Comprehension

This unit covers the following four comprehension skills:
- Main idea and supporting details
- Sequence
- Compare and contrast
- Cause and effect

Your students may already feel frustrated by language issues, lack of fluency, or inability to comprehend what they read. Before you begin the unit, try to move students' thinking beyond the classroom by showing them that reading is a life skill, not just a classroom skill.

Student page 7 ▶

| Main idea and supporting details |
| Sequence |
| Compare and contrast |
| Cause and effect |

Introducing the Unit

Refer students to the list of comprehension skills.

Have students read each skill aloud. To activate prior knowledge, ask students if they know the meaning of each skill. Then ask students for examples.
- Ask *Does anyone know the meaning of main idea?* Have volunteers share their responses with the class.
- Ask *Does anyone know the meaning of sequence?* Have volunteers share their responses with the class.
- Ask *Does anyone know the meaning of compare and contrast?* Have volunteers share their responses with the class.
- Ask *Does anyone know the meaning of cause and effect?* Have volunteers share their responses with the class.

Reinforce that students will learn about these skills and practice using them. Tell students that at the end of the unit they will have an opportunity to do a personal evaluation of what they learned.

In order to connect learning to their own lives, provide students with additional real-life examples of how they might be using comprehension skills.

Examples:

Main idea: telling what a book, movie, or TV show is about

Sequence: following directions for how to get to a friend's house; reading instructions about a game

Compare and contrast: choosing between two games by thinking about how they are alike and different; thinking about ways you and a friend are alike and different

Cause and effect: having a shoelace come untied, which makes you trip; oversleeping, which causes you to be late for school

At the End of the Unit

When students finish the skills in this unit, have them return to this page and check the box next to each skill. Then have them complete the exercise at the bottom of the page. In this activity, your students will reflect on the following three things:
- what they learned
- what they feel good about
- what they feel they need more practice with

This exercise makes learning personal and allows students to reflect on what they've learned. Ask students to be active learners. Help them understand that they are responsible for their own learning.

Objective

To identify the most important details in a passage as a way to understand the main idea. Using a variety of tools, students will learn to identify the main idea and supporting details and to answer questions about the main idea and supporting details.

Build Background

Say *When I read a book, it is important for me to understand the main idea, or what the story or passage is about. In the story "The Three Little Pigs," the author gives details about each pig building a house to keep the wolf out. The pig that used the strongest material had the house that kept the wolf out. So the main idea of the story was the pigs building their houses to keep the wolf out.*

Student page 8 ▶ **Learn the Skill**

Discuss with students the relationship between main idea and supporting details to see if they understand.

Coaching Tip

Point out to students that it may be helpful to find the details first to determine what the main idea is.

▶ **Apply the Skill**

Identifying the main idea and supporting details will help students understand what they read. In this section, students will learn and use tools to help them identify and answer questions about the main idea and supporting details.

- Have students read the following sentences as you write them on the board.
  Carmela and her family did many exciting things on their vacation. They swam in the ocean and went on rides at the state fair. Carmela and her brother Carlos ate lots of ice cream and popcorn at the fair, too. They had good memories of their exciting vacation.
- Ask *What is the main idea of the passage?* (Carmela and her family did many exciting things on their vacation.) Circle it and say *I circled the main idea of the passage.*
- Ask *What is one of the supporting details?* (swam in the ocean) Underline it and say *I underlined one of the supporting details in the passage.*
- Ask *What is another supporting detail?* (went on rides) Underline it and say *I underlined another supporting detail in the passage.* Continue in this manner.
- Have students read the next passage and circle the main idea and underline supporting details. Draw a main idea web on the board.
- Ask a volunteer to tell what he or she underlined and to explain his or her thinking. Redirect as necessary. Record the answers on the web. Repeat for the main idea.
- Have students compare your web to the one on page 9. Let them know that a main idea web is a way to organize details and the main idea. Also tell them they can draw a main idea web to help answer questions about supporting details and main ideas.

Student page 9
Answers

Paragraph 1

Supporting Details
took the train, visited grandfather at work, had lunch at a restaurant

Main Idea
Grandmother and I took a trip.

Paragraph 2

Supporting Details
visit the art and science museums, stroll through park, take train home

Main Idea
Grandmother and I are planning a trip for next month.

▶ **With a Partner**

Have students work together and discuss their thinking with each other and with the class.

- Have pairs of students read the passage. Instruct them not to fill in the main idea web for paragraph 1 in their books yet.
- Come back together as a class. Draw a blank web for paragraph 1 on the board.
- Say *I found a supporting detail for paragraph 1. We took the early train. Did you find it? Underline the sentence. I found another supporting detail for paragraph 1. We visited my grandfather at work. Did you find it? Underline it.*
- Fill in the web for paragraph 1 and have students copy these details into the web in their books.
- Have students circle the main idea of paragraph 2 and underline the supporting details. Then have them draw a main idea web and fill it in.
- Invite students to tell what they wrote in the web and explain their thinking. Redirect as necessary. Record the answers in the web on the board. Continue until all students have recorded all supporting details and the main idea.

▶ **On Your Own**

Ask students to work independently on a short practice test.

- Encourage students to circle the main idea, underline the supporting details, and draw a main idea web.
- Come back together as a class and ask them to explain their answer choices. Redirect as necessary.

Think About

Have students review the tools they've learned before beginning the On Your Own activity.

Differentiated Instruction

Answers

1. B
2. A
3. C

English Language Learners

Write these topics on the board: *States, Dogs,* and *Flowers.* Ask each student to come up with a more specific example for each topic. For example, *Texas* could be an example for *States.* After each student has narrowed the topic, have him or her choose one of the topics and write a main idea sentence for that topic. Each student should then add details that support the main idea.

Struggling Learners

Ask students to think about a celebration they recently attended. Ask a volunteer to tell the class about the celebration. Have classmates identify the important details and then the main idea of the story. Have students take turns.

Visual Learners

Have students use a highlighter to mark supporting details as they read the passage about Rida and Azim. This will help them to easily see the supporting details of the passage as they decide on the main idea.

Your Dictionary

Have students turn to page 252 and write or copy the definitions for *details* and *main idea* and give an example. (details—give more information about the main idea; main idea—what a passage or paragraph is about)

Objective

To understand the sequence of steps or events in a passage. Using a variety of tools, students will learn to identify the sequence in a passage and to answer questions about sequence.

Build Background

Say *When I make dinner, I often use a cookbook. The cookbook has recipes that tell me how to make things.* Read a simple recipe aloud. Then ask *What is the first step in this recipe? What is the second step?* Say *When you read a passage, look for the correct order of steps or events that occur in the passage to help you better understand what you are reading.*

Student page 11 ▶ **Learn the Skill**

Discuss with students the importance of identifying the order of steps in a passage.

Coaching Tip

Point out to students that it may be helpful for them to number the steps or events as they read the passage.

▶ **Apply the Skill**

Understanding and remembering the order of steps or events in a passage will help students understand what they read. In this section, students will learn and use tools to help them identify and answer questions about sequence.

- Write the following on the board. *To make a peanut butter and jelly sandwich, first spread the peanut butter on one piece of bread. Next spread the jelly on the other piece of bread. Then put the two pieces of bread together.*
- Ask *What happens first?* (You spread the peanut butter on one piece of bread.)
- Ask *What happens next?* (You spread the jelly on the other piece of bread.)
- Ask *What happens last?* (You put the two pieces of bread together.)
- Have students read the next passage and number the steps in the process. Draw an empty step chart on the board.
- Ask a volunteer to tell what she numbered as the first step and to explain her thinking. Redirect as necessary. Record the answer in the step chart. Repeat for all the steps.
- Have students compare your chart to the one on page 12 to see if they match. Let them know that a step chart is a way to organize the steps in a process. Also tell them that they can draw a step chart to help them answer questions about sequence.

Student page 12 ▶ **With a Partner**

Have students work together and discuss their thinking with each other and with the class.

- Have pairs of students read the passage. Tell them not to fill in the step chart in their books yet.
- Come back together as a class.
- Say *I found the first step.* First find several big pine cones. *Did you find it? Number the first step. I also found the second step.* Then roll the pine cones in peanut butter. *Do you see it? Number it.*
- Draw a chart on the board, fill it in, and have students copy the steps in the chart in their books.
- Have students look for steps 3 to 6. Remind them to number them. Then have them draw a step chart in their books and fill it in.
- Invite students to tell what they wrote in the chart and to explain their thinking. Redirect as necessary. Record the answers in the chart on the board. Continue until all students have recorded all of the steps in the process.

Answers

Step 1: *First find several big pine cones.* Step 2: *Then roll the pine cones in peanut butter.*
Step 3: *Next roll them in birdseed.* Step 4: *Tie a string to the top of each pine cone.* Step 5: *Now hang them in a tree.*
Step 6: *Finally watch the birds as they enjoy their food.*

▶ **On Your Own**

Ask students to work independently on a short practice test.

- Encourage students to number the various steps in the passage and to draw a step chart.
- Come back together as a class and have students explain their answer choices. Redirect as necessary.

Think About

Have students review the tools they have learned before beginning the On Your Own activity.

Differentiated Instruction

English Language Learners

Demonstrate the the sequence of steps for making a peanut butter and jelly sandwich by modeling how to make the sandwich.

Say *First the boy spread the peanut butter on one piece of bread.* Demonstrate this. *Then he spread the jelly on the other piece of bread.* Demonstrate this. *Then he put the two pieces of bread together.* Demonstrate this.

Ask *What is the first step in making a peanut butter and jelly sandwich?* Ask *What is the second step? The last step?* Write students' responses on the board.

Struggling Learners

Ask students to think about a time when they had to make or do something they do every day. Ask a volunteer to tell about the steps involved. Have classmates identify the steps. (Example: making their beds)

Kinesthetic Learners

Have students read the bird feeder passage and then make the bird feeder. Remind them to revisit the passage to keep track of the steps they have completed.

Answers

1. B
2. D
3. A

Your Dictionary

Have students turn to page 252 and write or copy the definition for *sequence* and give an example. (sequence—the order in which steps or events occur)

Objective

To use compare and contrast relationships to understand texts. Using a variety of tools, students will learn to compare and contrast people or objects in a passage, and to answer questions about compare and contrast.

Build Background

Place a tennis ball and a golf ball on your desk. Write *Compare* on the board. Ask *How are these two things alike?* Write answers such as *They are both balls; they are both round; they are both used in games.* Write *Contrast* on the board. Ask *How are these two things different?* Write answers such as *They are different colors, materials, and sizes; one is hit with a club, while the other is hit with a racket.* Tell students that when they compare two or more things, they find ways in which they are alike. When they contrast two or more things, they find ways in which they are different.

Student page 14 ▶ ## Learn the Skill

Discuss with students the difference between compare and contrast to be sure they understand it.

Coaching Tip

Point out to students that there may not always be an equal number of similarities and differences between two or more things.

▶ ## Apply the Skill

Knowing how to compare and contrast will help students understand what they read. In this section, students will learn and use tools to help them identify and answer questions about compare and contrast.

- Write on the board *Skateboards and in-line skates both have wheels. A skateboard has a flat board attached to the wheels, but in-line skates have boots attached to the wheels.*
- Ask *How are skateboards and in-line skates alike?* (Both have wheels.) Circle the words that show how they are alike. Say *I circled the way they are similar.*
- Ask *How are they different?* (A skateboard has a flat board, but in-line skates have boots.) Underline the words that show how they are different. Say *I underlined the ways they are different.*
- Have students cover up the chart in the book as they read the next passage and circle the similarities and underline the differences. Draw an empty compare and contrast diagram on the board.
- Ask a volunteer to tell what she circled and to explain her thinking. Redirect as necessary. Record the answer in the diagram. Repeat the procedure for contrast.
- Have students compare your diagram to the one in the book to see if they match. Tell them that the compare and contrast diagram is a way to organize compare and contrast. Also tell them that they can use a diagram to help them answer questions about compare and contrast.

Student page 15 ▶ ## With a Partner

Have students work together and discuss their thinking with each other and with the class.

Answers

Apples
1. red, green, or yellow
2. don't have to peel
3. Vitamin A

Oranges
1. orange
2. have to peel
3. Vitamin C

Both
1. types of fruit, grow on trees
2. taste sweet
3. good for you

- Have pairs of students read the passage. Tell them not to fill in the diagram in their books yet.
- Come back together as a class.
- Say *I found one way in which apples and oranges are alike.* They are a type of fruit. *Did you find it? Circle the words. I also found a way they are different.* Apples can be red, green, or yellow, but ripe oranges are always orange. *Do you see it? Underline it.*
- Draw a compare and contrast diagram on the board, fill it in, and have students copy the words in the diagram in their books.
- Have students find other examples of compare and contrast relationships in the passage. Remind them to circle the ways the things are alike and underline the ways they are different. Then have them add their answers to the diagram in their books.
- Invite students to tell what they wrote in their diagrams and to explain their thinking. Redirect as necessary. Record the answers in the diagram on the board. Continue until all students have recorded all compare and contrast relationships.

Ask students to work independently on a short practice test.
- Encourage students to circle and underline in the passage and to draw a compare and contrast diagram.
- Come back together as a class and ask students to explain their answer choices. Redirect as necessary.

Think About

Have students review the tools they've learned before beginning the On Your Own activity.

Answers

1. C
2. A
3. B

Differentiated Instruction

English Language Learners

Bring in pictures from sports magazines that illustrate different comparisons and contrasts from this passage. Examples would include pictures of a football and soccer ball, a soccer player kicking a goal, a receiver catching a pass, and others. Read the passage again with students and show the pictures to reinforce the comparison or contrast between the sports.

Struggling Learners

Invite students to compare and contrast something in their own life, such as two shirts they have at home, two dogs they saw at the park, or two games they like to play. Have students take turns doing this.

Visual Learners

Write several questions on the board for students to answer on a sheet of paper. Questions might include the following: *Where do you go to school? Where do you live? What hobbies do you have? What sports do you like? How many brothers and sisters do you have? What is your favorite color?* Have students work in pairs to share their answers. Then, on a large piece of paper, have the pairs of students draw a compare and contrast diagram. Ask each student to write his or her name in one of the circles. Have them write *Both* as a heading for the overlapping area. Tell students to write what they have in common in the overlapping circle and the other information under their own name. Ask students to display their diagrams to the class.

Your Dictionary

Have students turn to page 252 and write or copy the definitions for *compare* and *contrast* and give examples. (compare—to show how two or more things are alike; contrast—to show how two or more things are different)

Objective

To use cause and effect relationships to understand texts. Using a variety of tools, students will learn to identify the cause and the effect in a passage, and to answer questions about cause and effect.

Build Background

Drop a book on a table. Say *I dropped a book.* Ask *What happened?* (There was a loud noise.) *Why was there a noise?* (I dropped a book.) Say *The effect is something that happens because of a cause. The cause is what makes something happen. The loud noise is the effect. Dropping the book is the cause, or what caused the loud noise.*

Student page 17 ▶ **Learn the Skill**

Discuss with students the relationship between cause and effect to be sure they understand it.

Coaching Tip

Point out to students that sometimes it's easier to find the effect before finding the cause.

▶ **Apply the Skill**

Knowing what happens and why it happens will help students understand what they read. In this section, students will learn and use tools to help them identify and answer questions about cause and effect.

- Write on the board *Simone studied. She passed the math test.*
- Ask *What happened?* (Simone passed the test.) Underline it and say *I underlined the effect.*
- Ask *Why did she pass the test?* (because she studied) Circle it and say *I circled the cause.*
- Have students cover up the chart in the book as they read the next passage and underline the effect and circle the cause. Draw an empty chart on the board.
- Ask a volunteer to tell what he or she underlined and to explain his or her thinking. Redirect as necessary. Record the answer in the chart. Repeat for the cause.
- Have students compare your chart to the one in the book to see if they match. Let them know that the chart is a way to organize cause and effect. Also tell them they can draw a chart to help them answer questions about cause and effect.

Student page 18 ▶ **With a Partner**

Answers

Causes

1. Estela hoped she could get home before it rained.
2. Heavy raindrops began falling.
3. She began to run.
4. She was too late/it began raining.

Effects

1. She started walking quickly.
2. Estela put her books under her jacket.
3. She could reach the front door within seconds.
4. Estela was very wet.

Have students work together and discuss their thinking with each other and with the class.

- Have pairs of students read the passage. Tell them not to fill in the cause and effect chart in their books yet.
- Come back together as a class.
- Say *I found one effect.* Leaves on the nearby lawns were spinning in the air. *Did you find it? Underline the sentence. I also found the cause:* because the wind was blowing hard. *Do you see it? Circle it.*
- Draw a chart on the board, fill it in, and have students copy the cause and effect in the chart in their book.
- Have students look for other causes and effects in the passage. Remind them to underline the effects and circle the causes. Then have them draw a cause and effect chart in their book and fill it in.
- Invite pairs of students to tell what they wrote in the chart and to explain their thinking. Redirect as necessary. Record the answers in the chart on the board. Continue until all students have recorded all causes and effects.

▶ On Your Own

Ask students to work independently on a short practice test.

- Encourage students to circle and underline in the passage and to draw a cause and effect chart.
- Come back together as a class and ask students to explain their answer choices. Redirect as necessary.

Think About

Have students review the tools they've learned before beginning the On Your Own activity.

Answers

1. C
2. A
3. D

Differentiated Instruction

Struggling Learners

Ask students to think about something that happened to them today. Ask a volunteer to tell the class what happened. Have classmates identify cause and effect. Example: *I left my sneakers in the middle of my room* (cause). *I tripped over them* (effect).

English Language Learners

Model in stick figures the relationship between Estela and the rain. Draw a stick figure next to a picture of raindrops. Draw another stick figure standing in the rain. Beginning with the stick figure, say *Estela was walking home. It started to rain. She got wet.* Have students identify cause (rain) and effect (she got wet).

Visual Learners

Have students use two different colors to highlight the cause and the effect in the passage. Then have them highlight what happened and why it happened using corresponding colors in the cause and effect chart.

Your Dictionary

Have students turn to page 252 and write or copy the definitions for *cause* and *effect* and give examples. (cause—why something happens; effect—what happens as a result of the cause)

Answers

Hot Summer Days

1. A Incorrect. Paco never compares going to the beach to playing with water balloons.
   B Incorrect. Paco never mentions bringing Shaggy to the beach.
   C **Correct. Paco begs his mother to go to the beach and gives reasons why they should go.**
   D Incorrect. Paco does like to do these things, but they are supporting details, not the main idea of the paragraph.

2. A Incorrect. Paco can tell that going to the beach is not Mom's favorite idea, but this is not a detail that explains her reasons.
   B **Correct. Mom clearly says the beach will be crowded and that she hates crowds. She suggests making ice cream as a better idea.**
   C Incorrect. Mom does pat Paco on the head, but it does not tell us why she would rather make ice cream than go to the beach.
   D Incorrect. Mom suggests that making ice cream is a better idea than going to the beach, but she never says it is more fun.

3. A **Correct. Mom and Paco made ice cream to cool off on a hot day.**
   B Incorrect. This is not mentioned in the passage.
   C Incorrect. The passage doesn't talk about keeping Paco busy.
   D Incorrect. The passage does not contain information about the beach being closed.

4. A **Correct. This is stated in the first paragraph.**
   B Incorrect. This is not what Paco loves most about summer.
   C Incorrect. This is not stated in the passage.
   D Incorrect. Paco does not mention the ice cream truck as a reason why he loves summer.

5. A Incorrect. This is the first step.
   B Incorrect. This is the second step.
   C **Correct. This is the third step.**
   D Incorrect. This is the final step.

6. A Incorrect. According to paragraph 9, this is the last idea, and it is Mom's idea, not Paco's.
   B Incorrect. Paco does not suggest chasing Shaggy as a way to stay cool.
   C **Correct. This is Paco's first suggestion for staying cool.**
   D Incorrect. This is the second idea Paco has for staying cool.

7. A Incorrect. Paco's mom does not like hot weather.
   B Incorrect. Paco's mom does not like to go to the beach.
   C Incorrect. This shows how they are different, not alike.
   D **Correct. Both Paco and his mom like ice cream.**

8. A **Correct. This is stated in paragraph 1.**
   B Incorrect. Both Paco and his mom enjoy water balloon fights.
   C Incorrect. This answer shows how they are alike. It does not show how they are different.
   D Incorrect. Both Paco and his mom like banana ice cream.

Unit 2: Fiction and Nonfiction Skills

This unit covers the following seven fiction and nonfiction skills:

- Character
- Plot and setting
- Theme
- Literary elements
- Structural elements
- Visual information
- Nonfiction writing

You may need to explain to students that fiction stories are not true, and that nonfiction stories are about true events or actual things. Explain that in this unit students will learn skills that will help them better understand fiction stories and nonfiction writing.

Student page 22 ▶ **Introducing the Unit**

Character
Plot and setting
Theme
Literary elements
Structural elements
Visual information
Nonfiction writing

Refer students to the list of fiction and nonfiction skills.

Have students read each skill aloud. To activate prior knowledge, ask students if they know the meaning of each skill.

- Ask *Does anyone know the meaning of character?* Have volunteers share their responses with the class.
- Ask *Does anyone know the meaning of plot and setting?* Have volunteers share their responses with the class.
- Ask *Does anyone know the meaning of theme?* Have volunteers share their responses with the class.
- Ask *Does anyone know what a simile or metaphor is?* Have volunteers share their responses with the class.
- Ask *Does anyone know what a table of contents, heading, or index is?* Have volunteers share responses with the class.
- Ask *Does anyone know what a graphic is?* Have volunteers share responses with the class.
- Ask *Does anyone know different types of nonfiction writing?* Have volunteers share their responses with the class.

Reinforce that students will learn about these skills and practice using them. Tell students that at the end of the unit they will have an opportunity to do a personal evaluation of what they have learned.

Then ask students to share examples of each skill. In order to connect learning to their own lives, provide students with additional real-life examples of these skills.

Examples:

Character: Victor cleaned his room and threw out the trash. He is helpful.

Plot and setting: Jim gets lost in a store but is later found. The story takes place in New York in 1985.

Theme: Hard work is rewarded.

Literary elements: After he studied, Blair's grades went up like a rocket.

Structural elements: a table of contents, chapter titles, or a book's index

Visual information: a chart showing an airline schedule of flights

Nonfiction writing: step-by-step instructions on how to build a birdhouse

At the End of the Unit

When students finish the skills in this unit, have them return to this page and check the box next to each skill. Then have them complete the exercise at the bottom of the page. In this activity, your students will reflect on the following three things:

- what they learned
- what they feel good about
- what they feel they need more practice with

This exercise makes learning personal and allows students to reflect on what they've learned. Ask students to be active learners. Help them understand that they are responsible for their own learning.

Objective

To study character as a way to better understand texts. Using a variety of tools, students will learn to identify the characters in a passage and answer questions about them.

Build Background

- Write the following words on the board: *sad, angry, greedy, friendly, helpful.*
- Have students work in pairs. Have one student in each pair choose one of the words from the board and act it out. The partner tries to figure out which word was chosen.
- When each pair has completed the exercise, tell students that you might use these words to describe characters in a passage. Point out that just as they used clues to figure out which word their partners chose, they can also look for clues when they read.

Student page 23 ▶ **Learn the Skill**

Tell students that looking for clues will help them analyze characters in the stories they read.

Coaching Tip

Tell students that analyzing characters is like being a detective. First they look for clues, and then they try to figure out what the clues mean.

▶ **Apply the Skill**

Looking at what characters say and do will help students understand what they read. In this section students will learn and use tools to help them identify and answer questions about characters.

- Have students read the following sentences as you write them on the board. *Horace swept the floor. Then he swept the dirt under the sofa. "Good enough," he said.*
- Ask *What does the character say?* (He says his work is good enough.) Underline Horace's words. Say *I underlined the words the character said.*
- Ask *What does the character do?* (He sweeps the dirt under the sofa.) Circle Horace's actions. Say *I circled what the character did.*
- Have students cover up the chart in the book as they read the next passage and underline the words the character says and circle what the character does.
- Draw an empty character clues web on the board.
- Ask a volunteer to tell what he circled or underlined and to explain his thinking. Redirect as necessary. Record the answer in the boxes on the web. Repeat the procedure for each clue. Then ask *What kind of person would say or do these things?* Record answers in the circle of the web.
- Have students compare your web to the one in the book. Tell them that the two webs do not have to match because there are many ways to describe characters. Let them know that the web is one way to organize the clues about characters in a passage. Also tell them that they can draw a clues web to help them answer questions about characters.

Student page 24 ▶ **With a Partner**

Possible Answers

Ana's mother is—
1. kind
2. caring

Clues
1. put her arm around Ana
2. talked softly
3. gave Ana a hug
4. encouraged Ana

Have students work together and discuss their thinking with each other and with the class.

- Pair students and have them read the passage together. Tell them not to fill in the character clues web in their books yet.
- Come back together as a class. Draw a blank character clues web on the board.
- Say *I found one clue: "You'll be fine, Ana." Did you find it?* Underline the sentence. Say *I found one action: She put her arm around Ana to comfort her. Do you see it? Circle it.*
- Fill in the web on the board and have students copy the clues in their webs.
- Pair students again. Tell them that now they will draw their own clues web and fill it in.
- Invite students to tell what they wrote in their web and to explain their thinking. Redirect as necessary. Record the answers in the web on the board. Repeat the procedure until the web includes several clues and a corresponding character trait.

Think About

Have students review the tools they've learned before beginning the On Your Own activity.

Answers
1. B
2. C
3. C

▶ **On Your Own**

Ask students to work independently on a short practice test.
- Encourage students to circle and underline in the passage and to draw character clues webs in the margin.
- Come back together as a class and ask them to explain their answer choices. Redirect as necessary.

Differentiated Instruction

Struggling Learners

Invite one student to describe a person he or she knows or a character in a favorite movie or TV show. Encourage the student to quote statements made by the person and to mention things the person has done. Point out that these details are clues. Have classmates think of words to describe this person's character.

English Language Learners

For students having trouble understanding the relationship between clues and character traits, model the clues in pictures. Draw a stick figure lying in bed with bubbles leading up to a dream that shows the stick figure playing the violin. Point to the figure lying in bed. Say *Derek spent so much time dreaming that he did not practice his violin.* Ask *What kind of person is Derek?* Write student responses on the board.

Auditory Learners

Have students work in pairs to brainstorm things a family member says and what they do. Then they should say what kind of person would say and do those things. Example: *"Be careful crossing the street."* Character trait: *She is a caring mother.*

Your Dictionary

Have students turn to page 252 and write or copy the definition for *character* and give an example. (character—a person, animal, or make-believe creature in a story)

Objective

To use plot and setting to understand texts. Using a variety of tools, students will learn to recognize the plot and setting in a passage and to answer questions about plot and setting.

Build Background

Ask a volunteer to tell a short, familiar story. Have students identify the actions that happened in the story. Tell them that these actions are the plot. Have students identify where and when the story occurs. Tell them that this is the story's setting.

Student page 26 ▶ **Learn the Skill**

Identifying the actions that happen in a passage will help students analyze the plot. Determining where and when the actions occur will help students recognize the setting.

Coaching Tip

Point out to students that both the plot and setting of a story may change from the beginning to the end.

▶ **Apply the Skill**

Students will learn and use tools to help them identify and answer questions about plot and setting.

- Have students read the following sentences as you write them on the board. *LaToya sighed. She did not want to spend the afternoon cleaning. But her bedroom was a giant mess. She started putting things away. Later her room was spotless.*
- Ask *What happens in this passage?* (LaToya cleans her room.) Underline the actions. (*sighed* and *started putting things away*) Say *I underlined the action words.*
- Ask *Where does this passage take place?* (LaToya's bedroom) Circle the word *bedroom*. Ask *When does this passage take place?* (in the afternoon) Circle the word *afternoon*. Say *I circled the words that describe places and times.*
- Have students cover up the chart in the book as they read the next passage and underline the action words and circle words that describe the setting. Draw an empty plot and setting chart on the board.
- Ask a volunteer to tell you what she underlined and to explain her thinking. Redirect as necessary. Record the answers in the chart. Repeat for the setting.
- Ask a volunteer to tell you one of the actions he or she underlined. Record the answer in the chart on the board. Redirect as necessary. Repeat the procedure for each section of the plot.
- Have students compare your plot and setting chart to the one in the book to see if they match. Let them know that a plot and setting chart is one way to organize the plot and setting of a passage. Also tell them that they can draw a plot and setting chart to help them answer questions about plot and setting.

Student page 27 ▶ **With a Partner**

Answers

Plot
1. Esther squinted at the board.
2. Esther walked to the front of the room.
3. Esther walked back to her desk and squinted really hard.

Setting
1. school
2. classroom

Have students work together and discuss their thinking with each other and with the class.
- Pair students and have them read the passage together. Tell them not to fill in the plot and setting chart in their books yet.
- Come back together as a class. Draw a blank plot and setting chart on the board.
- Say *I found one action.* During her morning math class, Esther squinted at the board as she tried to copy the math problems. *Did you find it? Underline the sentence. I also found where the action takes place.* The room was quiet. *Do you see it? Circle it.*
- Fill in the chart on the board and have students copy the plot and setting in their own charts.
- Pair students again. Have them add plot and setting information to their charts. Have students look for other words that describe plot and setting in the passage. Remind them to underline the action words and circle the words that describe places and times.
- Invite students to tell what they wrote in the chart and to explain their thinking. Redirect as necessary. Record the answers in the chart on the board. Continue until all students have recorded the actions and the setting.

Think About

Have students review the tools they've learned before beginning the On Your Own activity.

▶ On Your Own

Ask students to work independently on a short practice test.

- Encourage students to circle and underline in the passage and to draw a plot and setting chart in the margin.
- Come back together as a class and ask them to explain their answer choices. Redirect as necessary.

Differentiated Instruction

Answers

1. B
2. B
3. C

Struggling Learners

Invite one student to tell a story of something that recently happened to him or her. Ask the student to repeat the actions and then the setting of the story. Example: *I was running in the park.* (setting) *It started to rain.* (action) *I got wet.* (action.)

English Language Learners

Ask students to draw a picture of where the passage takes place. Point out to students that the picture shows the setting of the passage. Then ask students to include in their drawing the things that Sapphire does, such as holding on to the climbing bars, falling off the climbing bars, and trying to communicate to the coach that she is hurt. Explain to students that the actions that Sapphire takes make up the plot of the passage.

Kinesthetic Learners

Have students stand in a semicircle facing one another. Ask three volunteers to act out events that the other students say aloud. Begin a story for the students and instruct them to add an event to the story. As events are added, the three students should act them out.

Your Dictionary

Have students turn to page 252 and write or copy the definitions for *plot* and *setting* and give examples. (plot—the events or action in a story; setting—where and when a story takes place)

Objective
To understand and identify themes in texts. Using a variety of tools, students will learn to identify the theme of a passage and to answer questions about theme.

Build Background
Pantomime learning a lesson. Walk in one direction, but look in another direction, talking to students. Bump into a wall or desk. Feign surprise and mild pain.
Say
I bumped into the wall!
I should watch where I'm going!
I learned my lesson!
Ask
What lesson did I learn?
Lesson: I learned to watch where I am going.
Say *We can learn lessons from our actions, but also from reading stories. Many stories teach lessons. The lessons characters learn in a passage, how a character changes, and the lessons we learn from reading the passages can help us identify the theme.*

Student page 29 ▶ **Learn the Skill**
Discuss with students how a theme is a message that the author is trying to tell you about life. Explain that the theme is usually not stated directly in the passage, but must be inferred from what the character learns or how the character changes in the passage.

Coaching Tip

Point out to students that finding the lesson the character learns will help them identify the theme.

▶ **Apply the Skill**
In this section, students will learn and use tools to help them identify and answer questions about theme.
- Have students read the following sentences as you write them on the board.
Susana was sick. She had a sore throat. Susana's mother tucked her in bed. She brought Susana some medicine. She sat by the bed until Susana fell asleep. When Susana woke up, she felt better.
- Ask *How does Susana change?* (She is sick and gets better.) Take notes in the margin to answer this question. Say *I took notes about Susana getting well.*
- Ask *What lesson about life can we all learn from the passage? A mother's care can help make us better.* Say *I wrote the theme in my own words.*
- Have students cover up the chart in the book as they read the next passage and take notes in the margin about how Marc changes and the lesson that Marc learns. Draw an empty theme chart on the board.
- Ask a volunteer to tell what he or she wrote in the margin about how Marc changes or the lesson that Marc learns and to explain his or her thinking. Redirect as necessary. Record the answers in the second column of the chart.
- Challenge students to brainstorm ideas about the theme suggested in the passage. Record their final wording in column 3 of the chart.
- Have students compare your chart to the one in the book to see if they match. Let them know that the chart is a way to organize lessons and themes from the passage. Also tell them that they can draw a chart to help them answer questions about theme.

Possible Answers

Character
Isabella
Change or Lesson
Isabella learned to be brave.
Theme
1. Being brave can help you make friends.
2. Being in a group is better than being alone.

With a Partner

Have students work together and discuss their thinking with each other and with the class.

- Pair students and have them read the passage together. Tell them not to fill in the theme chart in their books yet.
- Come back together as a class. Draw a blank chart on the board.
- Ask *Did you find the lesson that Isabella learned?* Encourage students to share their ideas and the notes they took in the margin that describe this lesson.
- Draw a chart on the board and fill it in. Have students copy the lesson in their chart.
- Have students identify and record one of the themes in their charts. *(Being brave can help you make friends.)*
- Invite students to tell what they wrote in the chart and explain their thinking. Redirect as necessary. Record the answers in the chart on the board.
- Explain to the class that a passage often has more than one theme.
- Continue until all students have recorded all the themes.

On Your Own

Ask students to work independently on a short practice test.

- Encourage students to take notes and draw a theme chart in the margins.
- Come back together as a class and ask students to explain their answer choices. Redirect as necessary.

Think About

Have students review the tools they've learned before beginning the On Your Own activity.

Answers

1. B
2. A
3. D

Differentiated Instruction

Struggling Learners

Invite groups of students to read stories with easily identifiable themes, such as fairy tales or picture books. Encourage them to share the stories with the class by reading or retelling them. Ask the class to identify the lesson the character learns or how the character changes. Then, together, list the themes of the passage. Encourage the students to record the lessons and themes discussed in a theme chart on the board.

English Language Learners

Invite students to tell about a funny event that happened to them recently. After individual students are finished telling their stories, ask them questions such as *What were you doing before that happened to you? Did the event change you in some way?* Tell students that the events that happen to us can teach us lessons.

Visual Learners

Have students draw pictures of the events from the passages. Encourage the students to connect their pictures to the themes of the passages.

Your Dictionary

Have students turn to page 252 and write or copy the definitions for *theme* and give one example.

Objective
To use literary elements to better understand texts. Using a variety of tools, students will learn to identify literary elements in a passage and to answer questions about literary elements.

Build Background
Read a poem.
Say *Poems use language in special ways to show feelings or images.*
Ask *What feelings or images did you hear in this poem?* Record the different elements students identify.
Say *You will learn how poems and stories use language in different ways to show feelings or images.*

Student page 32 ▶ **Learn the Skill**
Literary elements are used in stories and poems to create pictures or ideas in the reader's mind. Some elements that are used compare two very different things.

Coaching Tip

Remind students that to compare is to see how two things are similar.

▶ **Apply the Skill**
In this section, students will learn and use tools to help them identify and answer questions about literary elements.

- Have students read the following passage as you write it on the board.
  Jenna had a lot of homework to do. She was like a machine turning out the assignments. Finally it was time for bed. The pillow was a cloud on which she placed her tired head.
- Ask *What two things are being compared using the word* like? (Jenna and a machine) Underline these words. Say *I underlined the two things being compared using a simile.*
- Ask *What two things are being compared without using the words* like *or* as? (pillow and a cloud) Circle these words. Say *I circled the two things being compared using a metaphor.*
- Have students cover up the chart in the book as they read the next passage and underline the two things being compared using a simile and circle the things being compared using a metaphor. Draw an empty chart on the board.
- Ask a volunteer to tell what he or she underlined and to explain his or her thinking. Redirect as necessary. Record the answers in the second column of the chart. Repeat for the two other things being compared.
- Have students compare your chart to the one in the book to see if they match. Let them know that the chart is a way to organize literary elements from the passage. Also tell them that they can draw a chart to help them answer questions about literary elements.

Student page 33 ▶ **With a Partner**
Have students work together and discuss their thinking with each other and with the class.

- Pair students and have them read the passage together. Tell them not to fill in the simile and metaphor chart in their books yet.
- Come back together as a class.
- Say *I found a comparison:* Coach, like a dog, barks orders. *Did you find it? Underline the sentence.*
- Draw a chart on the board, fill it in, and have students copy the literary elements in their chart.
- Have students look for other comparisons in the passage. Remind them to underline the two things being compared. Then have them draw a literary elements chart in their books and fill it in.
- Invite pairs of students to tell what they wrote in the chart and to explain their thinking. Redirect as necessary. Record the answers in the chart on the board. Continue until all students have recorded all literary elements.

Answers
Literary Elements
Comparisons
Orange sun a ball
Coach, like a dog, barks orders.
Crouched like a tiger
Running now, I am an arrow.

On Your Own

Ask students to work independently on a short practice test.
- Encourage students to underline and circle in the passage and to draw a simile and metaphor chart in the margin.
- Come back together as a class and ask them to explain their answer choices. Redirect as necessary.

Think About

Have students review the tools they've learned before beginning the On Your Own activity.

Differentiated Instruction

Answers
1. B
2. A
3. A

Struggling Learners

Invite groups of students to act out the similes and metaphors in the passages. For example, students can pretend to be coaches barking out orders from the sideline or make sounds of train brakes that squeak like tree frogs.

English Language Learners

In two columns, write the following on the board. Write 4 or 5 similes and metaphors in random order in one column. In another column, write the words *simile* and *metaphor*. Remind students that similes use the words *like* or *as* to make a comparison and metaphors do not. Have volunteers come to the board and take turns drawing a line to connect each phrase to the word *simile* or *metaphor*. Encourage students to create more comparisons using similes or metaphors.

Visual Learners

Provide students with a different colored marker for each element. They can then see and understand each element as distinct. If possible, use colored chalks that match their markers to record each element in the chart on the board.

Your Dictionary

Have students turn to page 252 and write or copy the definitions for *simile* and *metaphor* and give an example for each. (simile—comparison between two objects using *like* or *as*; metaphor—comparison between two objects that does not use *like* or *as*)

Objective

To use structural elements to understand the content of text. Students will learn to identify the chapter titles, table of contents, headings, subheadings, and index when used in a text and to answer questions about them.

Build Background

Display a nonfiction book with a title that clearly tells what the book is about. Point to the title and ask students to read it aloud. Ask students what the title tells them and why the book's title is both necessary and helpful to the reader. Turn to the table of contents in the book and invite students to tell what it is and what it shows.

Student page 35 ▶ **Learn the Skill**

Discuss with students that to understand what they will read, it is helpful to understand the parts of a book or article.

Coaching Tip

Tell students to imagine that the title is a door that they are going to open. Based on what the title says, they should think of what will be inside.

▶ **Apply the Skill**

Knowing the structural elements of a book will help students understand what they read. In this section, students will learn and use tools to help them identify and answer questions about parts of a book.

- Have students read the table of contents. Ask *What is the title of the book?* (Home Improvement) *What do you think the book will be about?* (ways to make improvements in the home)
- Ask *What is the title of Chapter 1?* (Fixing Your Garage) *On what page does the chapter start?* (page 2)
- Have students read the passage. Ask *What is the heading?* (Building a Pool) *How does the heading help you know what you will read about?* (It tells what the following text will be about.)
- Ask *In which chapter would the passage be found?* (Chapter 2) *How do you know?* (Chapter 2 is about backyard projects, and a pool can be built in the backyard. The other chapters are about different kinds of home improvements.)

Student page 36 ▶ **With a Partner**

Have students work together and discuss their thinking with each other and with the class.

- Have pairs of students read the table of contents and fill in the labels in their books.
- Come back together as a class. Ask *What is the book title?* (Getting a Puppy) *What is the title of Chapter 2 and on what page does it start?* (Getting Your Home Ready, 7) *On what page does Chapter 1 start?* (3)
- Ask *Based on the information in the table of contents, what do you think the book will be about?* (what to do when you get a new puppy)
- Have pairs of students read the passage and answer the two questions that follow it.
- Come back together as a class and ask a volunteer to tell how he or she answered the questions.

Answers

1. Teaching Your Puppy
2. Chapter 3
3. The passage is about teaching and rules. The title of Chapter 3 mentions rules.

On Your Own

Ask students to work independently on a short practice test.

- Encourage students to think about what the titles and headings may be about.
- Come back together as a class and ask them to explain their answer choices. Redirect as necessary.

Differentiated Instruction

Answers

1. C
2. B
3. C

Struggling Learners

Ask students to imagine that they are getting a gift, a book titled *Card Tricks That Entertain.* Ask students to tell what they think the new book will be about. Repeat with other volunteers and titles.

English Language Learners

Show students several illustrated book covers while covering the book titles. Ask *What is this book about?* Invite students to write their own titles, based on the illustrations on the book covers.

Kinesthetic Learners

Find several short newspaper or magazine articles, cut them out, and separate the headings or titles from the articles. Glue each heading or title onto a separate index card or piece of paper. Then glue each article onto a separate piece of paper. Have the students match the article to its correct heading or title.

Your Dictionary

Have students turn to page 252 and write or copy the definitions for *table of contents, index, heading,* and *subheading* and give an example of each.

Objective

To use various graphics to understand information. Students will learn to use pictures, charts, time lines, diagrams, maps, and graphs to answer questions about visual information.

Build Background

Write *Some students have brothers and sisters* on the board. Take an informal poll of students to find out how many of them have a brother or sister, and if they do, how many of each they have. Create a chart listing *Sister* and *Brother* in two columns and *Number of Students* for each in the third column. Discuss how the completed chart offers more description than the sentence does.

Student page 38 ▶ **Learn the Skill**

Discuss with students the use of visual information to be sure they understand its importance.

Coaching Tip

Tell students to ask themselves "What is this graphic trying to tell me?" as they look at each one for the first time.

Apply the Skill

Visual information will help students understand what they read. In this section, students will learn and use tools to help them identify and answer questions about visual information.

- Have students read the chart title as you draw a chart and write the title, "Global Airlines," on the board.
- Have students read the information in the chart.
- Ask a volunteer to explain what she learned from the chart.
- Have students cover up the time line in their book as they read the passage.
- Have students uncover the time line, read the information, and answer the questions.
- Invite a volunteer to explain what he or she learned from the time line. Redirect as necessary. As a class, answer the questions that follow the diagram.
- Tell students that graphics are a way to organize information that may or may not be found in a passage.

Answers

1. The town picnic will take place at 2:00 P.M.
2. The town parade will take place at 12 noon.

Student page 39 ▶ **With a Partner**

Have students work together and discuss their thinking with each other and with the class.

- Have pairs of students read the passage. Then come back together as a class.
- Have students work in pairs to read the diagram and follow the steps to make a paper airplane. Then have students answer the questions after the diagram with their partners.
- Invite students to share their answers with the class and to explain their thinking. Redirect as necessary.

Answers

The diagram gives instructions on how to make a paper airplane.

The passage tells about the history of paper airplanes.

▶ **On Your Own**

Ask students to work independently on a short practice test.

- Encourage students to think about what the time line is telling them.
- Come back together as a class and ask them to explain their answer choices. Redirect as necessary.

Think About

Have students review the tools they've learned before beginning the On Your Own activity.

Answers

1. B
2. C
3. B

Differentiated Instruction

Struggling Learners

Have students construct a simple time line for their day at school. Have them fill in the time line with their activities and take turns explaining their time line to the class. Guide students with questions about their schedule during certain times of the day to reinforce their ability to read a chart.

English Language Learners

Create a chart titled *Favorite School Subjects*. The left column heading will be *Subject*, with a list of three or four different subjects. The right column heading will be *Favorite*. Take a poll in class and write the number of students next to the subject under the *Favorite* column. Ask a volunteer to look at the chart and describe what the chart says.

Kinesthetic Learners

Bring in advertisements from the grocery store or a magazine about food. Ask students to cut out pictures of their favorite foods. On a large poster board, draw a chart with each student's name in one column and the heading "Favorite Food" in another column. Invite students to glue the picture of their favorite food in each row. Tally up responses on the board, modeling how to read the chart.

Your Dictionary

Have students turn to page 252 and write or copy the definitions for *graphics* and *chart* and give an example. (graphics–give information that is not found in a passage; chart–a graphic that organizes information in rows and columns)

Objective

To understand the different types of nonfiction writing and each of their purposes. Using a variety of tools, students will learn to identify the purpose of nonfiction writing.

Build Background

Write these sentences on the board:

1. *On May 1, 1852, Martha Jane Cannary was born in Princeton, Missouri.*
2. *Jane stretched and yawned. It was not yet daylight.*

Read the sentences aloud. Ask *Which sentence gives facts?* (1) *Which reads like a story?* (2) Write *Nonfiction* after sentence 1 and *Fiction* after sentence 2. Read aloud the labels. Explain that nonfiction writing gives facts or information about real people, places, and events. Fiction is something made up by the writer. Provide some examples of nonfiction books for students to look at.

Student page 41 ▶ **Learn the Skill**

Explain to students that nonfiction writing is read for information and includes biographical, persuasive, functional, and informative writing. Explain the purpose of each type of nonfiction writing. Ask volunteers to read the descriptions from the chart.

Coaching Tip

Tell students to look for headings, facts, charts, and graphs when reading a passage. These are clues that the writing is nonfiction.

▶ **Apply the Skill**

In this section, students will learn and use tools to help them identify the different types of nonfiction writing and each type's purpose.

- Write on the board *The Pony Express was started to speed up sending mail between Missouri and California.*
- Ask *What is this passage about?* (the Pony Express) Underline it and say *I underlined the topic.*
- Write the following questions on the board:
  Is the writing telling me about someone's life? Write *no* next to the question.
  Is the writing trying to persuade me? Write *no* next to the question.
  Is the writing explaining how to do something? Write *no* next to the question.
  Is the writing informing me? Write *yes* next to the question.
- Have students cover up the chart in the book as they read the next passage on page 42 and underline the topic. Draw an empty chart on the board.
- Ask a volunteer to tell what she underlined and to explain her thinking. Redirect as necessary. Record the answer in the chart.
- Have students compare your chart to the one in the book to see if they match. Let them know that the chart is a way to organize nonfiction writing. Also tell them they can draw a chart to help them answer questions about nonfiction writing.

Student page 42 ▶ **With a Partner**

Have students work together and discuss their thinking with each other and with the class.

- Have pairs of students read the passage. Tell them not to fill in the nonfiction writing purpose chart in their books yet.
- Come back together as a class.
- Say *I know what the passage is about. It's about Samuel Morse. I read the questions and answered them by circling* yes *or* no. *The answer to the first question is yes, so I circled* yes. Invite students to tell what they circled for the rest of the questions.
- Have students circle the appropriate *yes* and *no* answers on their own charts.
- Have students discuss another purpose for the writing. Invite pairs of students to tell what they chose as a second purpose and have them explain their thinking. Redirect as necessary.

Answers

Purposes: biography and informative

chart on page 42.

Think About

Have students review the tools they've learned before beginning the On Your Own activity.

Answers

1. B
2. D
3. A

▶ **On Your Own**

Ask students to work independently on a short practice test.

- Encourage students to underline in the passage and refer back to the nonfiction writing chart on page 42.
- Come back together as a class and ask students to explain their answer choices. Redirect as necessary.

Differentiated Instruction

English Language Learners

Ask students to write or tell about an event that they remember from their own lives, an advertisement they recently saw, something they recently learned about, or something they recently learned to make or do. Remind students to include as much detail as they can. Encourage students to design a book cover for their story. Ask volunteers to share their stories with the class. Ask students to identify the types of nonfiction writing they have done.

Struggling Learners

Pair struggling learners with proficient readers and provide them with a nonfiction passage to read together. Have them work together to identify the purpose of the nonfiction writing. Remind them that a passage can have more than one purpose.

Kinesthetic Learners

Set up four areas in the classroom, one for each type of nonfiction writing. Choose a very short passage from a book or make up your own and read or say it aloud. Ask students to move to the area that corresponds to the type of passage you read. For example, if you read a persuasive passage, students who are able to identify the passage as persuasive would move to that area in the classroom.

Your Dictionary

Have students turn to page 252 and write or copy the definitions for *biography, persuasive writing, functional writing,* and *informative writing.* (biography—a true life story; informative writing—gives information and facts about a topic; persuasive writing—tries to convince the reader about something; functional writing—step-by-step directions or instructions)

Answers

Making the Team

1. A Incorrect. This is not the main theme.
   B Incorrect. Mia is actually learning to play basketball.
   C **Correct. This is the theme of the story. Mia's brother supported Mia by teaching her how to play basketball so that she could join the team.**
   D Incorrect. The passage does not state this.

2. A Incorrect. The text does not indicate that she is carefree. Paragraph 1 states that she is *upset.*
   B Incorrect. There is no evidence that she is funny.
   C **Correct. Mia is very determined. She tries even when she is not doing well.**
   D Incorrect. She is upset for most of the passage. At the end, she *felt better.* But *happy* does not describe her best.

3. A **Correct. Paragraph 2 states that Perry *came out of their house.***
   B Incorrect. Basketball camp is never mentioned.
   C Incorrect. A team practice is never mentioned or indicated.
   D Incorrect. A hospital is never mentioned or indicated.

4. A Incorrect. Mia plays with a ball but not with a child, so this is not a reason for the comparison.
   B Incorrect. Although a ball is used to play sports, a naughty child has nothing to do with it, so this is not a reason for the comparison.
   C **Correct. The ball is not doing what Mia is telling it to do, just like a naughty child might not do what someone tells him or her to do. This is the reason for the comparison.**
   D Incorrect. Mia talks to the ball but not to a child, so this is not a reason for the comparison.

Gerbils as Pets

5. A Incorrect. The title specifically mentions gerbils, not just animals.
   B **Correct. The title tells us that this will be the subject.**
   C Incorrect. The title does not mention the time needed to care for a gerbil.
   D Incorrect. The title does not mention ways to care for a gerbil.

6. A Incorrect. The time line shows that gerbils were used only for research in 1954.
   B Incorrect. Gerbils were available as pets in the 1960s, before 1980.
   C Incorrect. The year 1995 is not mentioned in the time line, and the time line shows that gerbils were used as pets in the 1960s.
   D **Correct. Gerbils began to be used as pets in the 1960s.**

7. A Incorrect. It does not try to convince the reader to buy a gerbil.
   B Incorrect. It does not teach the reader how to take care of gerbils.
   C **Correct. It does provide facts about gerbils.**
   D Incorrect. It does not entertain the reader with a funny story about gerbils.

Unit 3: Vocabulary

This unit covers the following four vocabulary skills:
- Root words, prefixes, and suffixes
- Synonyms and antonyms
- Context clues
- Multiple-meaning words

Before you begin the unit, have a discussion with students about the power of words. Point out that sentences, stories, and books are all just collections of words. Explain that the more words they know, the better they will be able to read. Then tell students that in this unit they will practice some skills that will help them learn new words.

Student page 46 ▶ ## Introducing the Unit

Refer students to the list of vocabulary skills.

Have students read each skill aloud. To activate prior knowledge, ask students if they know the meaning of each skill. Then ask students for examples.

> Root words, prefixes, and suffixes
> Synonyms and antonyms
> Context clues
> Multiple-meaning words

- Ask *Does anyone know the meaning of root words, prefixes, and suffixes?* Have volunteers share their responses with the class.
- Ask *Does anyone know the meaning of synonyms and antonyms?* Have volunteers share their responses with the class.
- Ask *Does anyone know how to find the meaning of an unknown word in a passage?* Have volunteers share their responses with the class.
- Ask *Does anyone know a word that can have different meanings?* Have volunteers share their responses with the class.

Reinforce that students will learn about these skills and practice using them. Tell students that at the end of the unit they will have an opportunity to do a personal evaluation of what they have learned.

In order to connect learning to their own lives, provide students with additional real-life examples of how they might be using vocabulary skills.

Examples:

Root words, prefixes, and suffixes: The prefix *un-* means "not," so *unhappy* means "not happy."

Synonyms and antonyms: A synonym for *big* is *large.* An antonym for *big* is *small.*

Context clues: *It is absurd to think that cows can fly.* You can understand the meaning of *absurd* from the rest of the sentence.

Multiple meaning words: The word *can* means "able to" and "sealed container."

At the End of the Unit

When students finish the skills in this unit, have them return to this page and check the box next to each skill. Then have them complete the exercise at the bottom of the page. In this activity, your students will reflect on the following three things:
- what they learned
- what they feel good about
- what they feel they need more practice with

This exercise makes learning personal and allows students to reflect on what they've learned. Ask students to be active learners. Help them understand that they are responsible for their own learning.

Objective

To identify root words, prefixes, and suffixes. Using a variety of tools, students will identify how prefixes and suffixes alter the meaning of root words. Students will understand new words by understanding their parts.

Build Background

Write *disagree* on the board. Say *Suppose you did not know this word. How could you figure out its meaning? Here is a plan. First look for a whole word in this word.* Help students identify *agree*. Say *The word* agree *is a root word. It is like the root of a plant. We can add word parts to it to "grow" new words.* Circle *dis.* Say *This is a word part added before a root word. It is a prefix. The prefix* dis- *means "not."* Elicit that *dis- + agree = disagree,* meaning "not agree."

Student page 47 ▶ **Learn the Skill**

Discuss with students that root words form the base of other words. Prefixes and suffixes are word parts added to root words to change their meanings.

Coaching Tip

Remind students to look for a root word, then for a prefix or suffix.

Apply the Skill

In this section, students will identify prefixes, root words, and suffixes in target words.
- Have students read the following sentences as you write them on the board. *Mars is unlike Earth. Mars is cold and airless.*
- Draw a box around *unlike.*
- Ask students to name the root word. Underline *like* as students respond.
- Say *The word part* un- *is added before* like, *so it is a prefix. The chart shows that* un- *means "not." That prefix changes the meaning of the root word. The new word* unlike *means "not like."* Circle *un-.* Say *I circled* un- *because it is a prefix.*
- Follow the same procedure for *airless.* Circle *less* and note that it is a suffix that means "without." Say *Airless means "without air."*
- Have students read the next passage, underline root words, and circle prefixes and suffixes. Draw an empty chart on the board like the chart on page 48.
- Ask volunteers to tell what they underlined as root words, what they circled as prefixes, and what they circled as suffixes. Record their answers in the chart on the board. Redirect as necessary.
- Have students compare the filled-in chart on the board with the one in the book to see if they match. Tell them that making a chart of word parts is a good way to learn and understand word meanings.

Student page 48 ▶ **With a Partner**

Have students work together and discuss their thinking with each other and with the class.

Answers

success/-ful/full of
    success
un-/believe/-able
    cannot be believed
dis-/cover/to learn of
un-/known/not known
un-/inviting/not
    inviting
harm/-ful/full of harm
life/-less/without life

- Have pairs of students read the passage. Tell them not to fill in the chart in their books yet.
- Come back together as a class. Draw a blank prefix, root word, suffix, and meaning chart on the board.
- Say *In the first shaded word, I see the root word* success. *Underline this word. I also see the suffix* -ful. *Circle it.*
- Pair students again. Have them find the remaining shaded words in the passage. Remind them to underline the root words and circle the prefixes and suffixes.
- Ask students to draw a prefix, root word, suffix, and meaning chart and fill it in.
- Invite pairs of students to the board to draw and fill in their charts. Redirect as necessary.

On Your Own

Ask students to work independently on a short practice test.

- Encourage students to underline and circle word parts in the passage and to draw a prefix, root word, suffix, and meaning chart.
- Come back together as a class and ask students to explain their answer choices. Redirect as necessary.

Think About

Have students review the tools they've learned before beginning the On Your Own activity.

Answers

1. A
2. D
3. B

Differentiated Instruction

Struggling Learners

Using index cards, make cards for common prefixes, suffixes, and root words. Color code them so that each type of word part is the same color. Have students work in pairs to see how many words they can form by combining the parts. Ask them to list the words they made. Have them check the words in a dictionary.

English Language Learners

Tell students that learning root words, prefixes, and suffixes will give them the tools they need to figure out many English words. Suggest that students make a word book for new words they learn. In one section they could write a root word at the top of the page, and under it they could write words in that root's "family" as they come across them in their reading.

Visual Learners

Have students use two different colored highlighters to highlight prefixes and suffixes. Have them use the same colors to indicate prefixes and suffixes as they complete the lesson.

Your Dictionary

Have students turn to page 252 and write or copy the definitions for *root word*, *prefix*, and *suffix*. For each one, have them give an example word that contains that word part. In the example, have them underline the root word and circle a prefix or a suffix.

Objective
To recognize that synonyms are words with similar meanings and antonyms are words that have opposite meanings.

Build Background
Write these sentences on the board.

The crowd was hushed and quiet before the show.
The game was exciting, not dull.

Read the sentences aloud. Point to *hushed* in the first sentence and say *Suppose you came to this word and did not know its meaning. Do you see any other words in the sentence that help you find its meaning?* Help students see that *quiet* is a synonym for *hushed.* It has a similar meaning.

Continue the same procedure for the second sentence. Help students see that *exciting* and *dull* have opposite meanings. They are antonyms.

Say *When authors use a new word, they sometimes follow it with a synonym or antonym that will show readers what it means. Look for synonyms and antonyms to help you figure out the meanings of words you see in your reading.*

Student page 50 ▶ **Learn the Skill**
Synonyms are words with similar meanings. Antonyms are words that have opposite meanings.

▶ **Apply the Skill**
Students will learn to use tools to help them identify synonyms and antonyms.

Coaching Tip
Tell students to think about the meaning of the sentence that contains a word they do not know. Tell students to look for words that might mean the same as or opposite of the word they do not know.

- Have students read the following sentences as you write them on the board. *The doctor said the illness was rare. It was not common. She said I would feel every ache and pain for a few days.*
- Point to *ache.* Say *Suppose I'm not sure what this word is. It's followed by* pain. *That could be a synonym.* Ache *means almost the same thing as* pain. Ache *and* pain *are synonyms.* Circle them. Say *I circled the synonyms.*
- Follow the same procedure for the antonyms *rare* and *common.* Underline them. Say *I underlined the antonyms.*
- Have students read the next passage, circle the synonyms, and underline the antonyms while you draw an empty synonym and antonym chart on the board.
- Ask a volunteer to tell which words he or she circled as synonyms, which words he or she underlined as antonyms, and why. Record his or her answers in the chart on the board. Redirect as necessary.
- Have students compare the filled-in chart on the board to the one in the book. Have them make sure the charts match. Tell them that making a synonym and antonym chart is a good way to learn and understand word meanings.

Student page 51 ▶ **With a Partner**

Answers

Synonyms
ocean — sea
race — contest
fly — soar
wee — small, little

Antonyms
quickest — slowest
rapidly — slowly

Have students work together and discuss their thinking with each other and with the class.

- Have pairs of students work together to fill in the synonym and antonym chart in their books after reading the passage.
- Come back together as a class. Draw a blank synonym and antonym chart on the board.
- Call on volunteers to tell what pair of words they wrote in the chart under *synonyms* and why, and what pair they wrote under *antonyms* and why.
- Record students' answers in the chart on the board. Redirect as necessary.
- Have students look for three more pairs of synonyms and one more pair of antonyms in the passage. Then have students add these words to the chart in their books.
- Invite pairs of students to the board to draw and fill in the synonym and antonym chart from their books. Redirect as necessary.

Ask students to work independently on a short practice test.

- Encourage students to circle and underline directly in the passage and to draw synonym and antonym charts in the margin.
- Have students regroup as a class and explain their answer choices. Redirect as necessary.

Differentiated Instruction

Struggling Learners

Have students use index cards to make flash cards for synonyms and antonyms. For a synonym, they would write a word in color on one side of a card and a synonym on the reverse side in the same color. For an antonym, they would write a word and its antonym in different colors. Have students use their cards in a game with another player.

English Language Learners

Pair ELL students with those proficient in English and have them make word books of synonyms and antonyms. You might wish to give them a category to start with, such as *size*. Suggest that they illustrate their entries. Make this an ongoing activity. Students could add words independently as they learn them.

Kinesthetic Learners

Have pairs of students act out synonym pairs and say what they are doing: *I am walking; I am strolling.* Then have them act out antonyms: *I am throwing; I am catching.*

Think About

Have students review the tools they've learned before beginning the On Your Own activity.

Answers

1. C
2. B
3. A

Your Dictionary

Have students turn to page 252 and write or copy the definitions for *synonym* and *antonym* and give one example. (synonym — a word that has a similar meaning to another word; antonym — a word that has an opposite meaning of another word)

Objective

To use context clues to decipher the meanings of unfamiliar words. Using a variety of tools, students will learn to identify context clues in a passage and answer questions about context clues.

Build Background

Show students a picture of a chef in a restaurant.

Ask *Who is the person in the picture?* Write *a chef* on the board. Ask *What clues help you figure out who this person is?* Write sentences on the board, such as *The person is wearing a chef's hat. The person is stirring a big pot on a restaurant stove.*

Say *You can find clues when you read to help you figure out the meaning of a word you do not know, in the same way you found clues about the person in the picture even though you did not know anything about the person.*

Student page 53 ▶ **Learn the Skill**

Knowing how to find context clues around an unfamiliar word will help students decipher its meaning and understand what they read.

Coaching Tip

Point out to students that they can write down what they think a word might mean based on what the sentence is telling them. They can use a dictionary to check the word's definition.

Apply the Skill

Students will learn and use tools to help them identify context clues to decipher unfamiliar words.

- Have students read the following sentences as you write them on the board. *Maria's puppy is very friendly. He will nudge you with his nose when he wants something from you.*
- Underline the word *nudge.* Say *I underlined the word* nudge.
- Ask *What clues help you define* nudge? (*with his nose, wants something from you*) Circle the context clues. Say *I circled the context clues.*
- Have students cover up the clues chart in the book as they read the next passage, find the unfamiliar word, and circle the context clues. Draw an empty clues chart on the board.
- Ask a volunteer to tell what clue helped to figure out the meaning of the underlined word. Have the student explain his or her thinking. Redirect as necessary. Record the answer in the chart. Complete the rest of the chart.
- Have students compare your chart to the one in the book to see if they match. Let them know that the chart is a way to organize the context clues. Also tell them that they can draw a chart to help them find context clues to define new words.

Student page 54 ▶ **With a Partner**

Have students work together and discuss their thinking with each other and with the class.

- Have pairs of students read the passage. Tell them not to fill in the clues chart in their books yet. Encourage them to discuss their thinking with each other.
- Come back together as a class. Draw a blank clues chart on the board.
- Say *I found a new word:* attempt. *Did you find it? The word is underlined. I also found some context clues: to jump, not be able to do it. Do you see them? Circle them. What is my reasoning?* (*The clues say you would not be able to jump as far as a kangaroo.*) *What is the definition of* attempt? (try)
- Fill in the chart on the board and have students copy what you wrote in their chart.
- Pair students again. Have them look for the other underlined words. Remind them to circle the context clues.
- Ask students to draw a clues chart in their books and fill it in.
- Invite pairs of students to tell what they wrote in the chart and to explain their reasoning. Redirect as necessary. Record the answers in the chart on the board. Continue until all students have recorded all the unfamiliar words, context clues, their reasoning, and definitions. (*leap*—clue: *jump up to 30 feet,* reasoning: *The red kangaroo can jump very far at one time,* meaning: *a long jump; graze*—clue: *stay in open fields, on grass,* reasoning: *The kangaroos stay in fields eating grass,* meaning: *to eat*)

► **On Your Own**

Ask students to work independently on a short practice test.

- Encourage students to circle in the passage and to draw a clues chart.
- Come back together as a class and ask them to explain their answer choices. Redirect as necessary.

Think About

Have students review the tools they've learned before beginning the On Your Own activity.

Differentiated Instruction

Answers

1. B
2. C
3. A

Struggling Learners

Ask students to find unfamiliar words in one of their books. Ask a volunteer to write one of the words on the board. Have classmates offer clues to the meaning of the word.
Example: *necklace*, possible clues: *a piece of jewelry, something you wear around your neck, a locket.*

English Language Learners

For students having trouble finding context clues, model on the board the relationship between the unfamiliar word *leap* and its clues. Write the word *leap* at the top of the board. Ask students to read the sentence in which *leap* appears. Ask them what the sentence says about the red kangaroo. Write students' responses under the word *leap*. Tell them that the words around *leap* are the context clues. Tell them that the context clues give the definition of the word *leap*.

Auditory Learners

Have students think of a secret word. Then have them write two sentences that tell about the secret word. (Example: For *soap*, students could write *Soap is something that you use to wash your hands.*) Then have students draw a line through the secret word in each sentence and write the word *blank* above it. Have the student read his or her sentences to the class, substituting *blank* in place of the secret word. Have the rest of the students guess the secret word.

Your Dictionary

Have students turn to page 252 and write or copy the definition for *context clues* and give an example. (context clues—words that you know that help you figure out the meaning of an unknown word)

Objective
To define multiple-meaning words. Students will learn which definition to use for multiple-meaning words they find in a passage and to answer questions about multiple-meaning words.

Build Background
Show students a picture of a green circle and a picture of a boy coloring. Hold up the first picture and say *My favorite color is green.* Hold up the second picture and say *Bill is going to color the picture.* Say *Some words have more than one meaning. They are called multiple-meaning words.*

Student page 56 ▶ **Learn the Skill**

Discuss with students how to figure out which definition to use for multiple-meaning words to be sure they understand it.

Coaching Tip

Point out to students that some multiple-meaning words are pronounced differently when they mean different things; for example, *bow* (bou) and *bow* (bo).

▶ **Apply the Skill**

In this section, students will learn and use tools to help them figure out which definition to use for multiple-meaning words.
- Write these sentences on the board. *Jill is serious about running on the track team. She uses a chart to track the times she spends practicing.*
- Ask *Which word has more than one meaning?* (track) Underline *track.* Say *I underlined* track. *Track has more than one meaning.*
- Ask *What are the two meanings of the word* track? ("a kind of sport" and "to observe the progress of something")
- Ask *What helped you decide which meaning to use?* Circle *running* and *chart.*
- Have students cover up the chart in the book as they read the next passage. Draw an empty chart on the board.
- Ask a volunteer to explain his or her thinking in selecting a meaning for the underlined word. Redirect as necessary. Record the answer in the chart.
- Have students compare your chart to the one in the book to see if they match. Let them know that the chart is a way to organize meanings of multiple-meaning words. Also tell them that they can draw a chart to help them find the right meanings for the underlined words.

Student page 57 ▶ **With a Partner**

Have students work together and discuss their thinking with each other and with the class.
- Have pairs of students read the passage. Tell them not to fill in the chart in their books yet.
- Come back together as a class. Draw a blank multiple-meaning word chart on the board.
- Say *I found a multiple-meaning word:* raise. *Did you find it? The word is underlined. What is one meaning of* raise? (to lift) *Another meaning?* (to increase in pay)
- Have students look at the other multiple-meaning words. Then have them draw a multiple-meaning word chart and fill it in.
- Invite students to tell what they wrote in the chart and explain their reasoning. Redirect as necessary. Record the answers in the chart on the board. Continue until all students have recorded all multiple-meaning words.

Answers

Word
1. *raise*
2. *tire*
3. *shape*

One Meaning
1. lift up
2. wheel on a vehicle
3. the form of something

Another Meaning
1. increase in pay
2. lose energy
3. to make

Ask students to work independently on a short practice test.
- Encourage students to think about which meanings make sense and to draw a multiple-meaning word chart.
- Come back together as a class and ask them to explain their answer choices. Redirect as necessary.

Think About

Have students review the tools they've learned before beginning the On Your Own activity.

Answers
1. C
2. A
3. D

Differentiated Instruction

English Language Learners

For students having trouble understanding multiple-meaning words, model the skill using a word map for *tire* and a word map for *shape*.

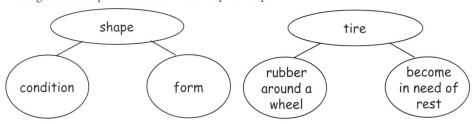

Say *You want your bike to be in good shape so it won't break down.* Point to the word *condition.* Say *That refers to the condition of the bike.* Point to the word *form.* Say *The shape of the seat refers to its form. It is long and narrow or short and wide.*
Say *The tire on your bike is the rubber part filled with air.* Point to the words *the rubber around a wheel.* Point to the words *become in need of rest.* Say *If you ride your bike for a long time, you might tire and need a break.*
Explain that the words have two different meanings. Tell students that some words may have several different meanings.

Struggling Learners

Give students a list of multiple-meaning words and a dictionary. Tell them they will be the "word experts" for these multiple-meaning words. Have them find the definitions for the words. Ask them to share the definitions they associate with the word and then to explain to the class the lesser-known definitions. As a class, try to use the lesser-known definition in sentences.

Visual Learners

Use pictures and demonstrations to present a series of multiple-meaning words. For example, show students a picture of a baseball bat. Then show a picture of an animal bat.

Your Dictionary

Have students turn to page 252 and write or copy the definition for *multiple-meaning words* and give an example. (multiple-meaning words—words that have more than one meaning)

Answers

An Entertaining Day

1. A Incorrect. *Paint* is not an antonym for *assemble.*
   B Incorrect. *Fly* is not an antonym for *assemble.*
   C **Correct. *Assemble* means "put together," so *take apart* means the opposite of *assemble.***
   D Incorrect. *Take down* is not an antonym for *assemble.*

2. A Incorrect. This answer does not give the correct meaning of the word *cheerful.* The root word *cheer* does not mean "tired," and the suffix *-ful* does not mean "again."
   B Incorrect. This answer does not give the correct meaning of the word *cheerful.* The root word *cheer* does not mean "fear," and the suffix *-ful* does not mean "without."
   C **Correct. This answer tells the meaning of the parts of the word *cheerful* (the suffix *-ful* means "full of," and the root word *cheer* means "happiness").**
   D Incorrect. This answer does not give the correct meaning of the word *cheerful.* The root word *cheer* does not mean "calm," and the suffix *-ful* does not mean "not."

3. A Incorrect. The word *color* does not have the same meaning, so it is not a synonym for *shape.*
   B **Correct. The words *shape* and *form* have the same meaning.**
   C Incorrect. The word *worth* does not have the same meaning, so it is not a synonym for *shape.*
   D Incorrect. The word *order* does not have the same meaning, so it is not a synonym for *shape.*

4. A Incorrect. *Fabulous* does not refer to size.
   B **Correct. *Wonderful* means the same as *fabulous.***
   C Incorrect. *Wild* is not the same as *fabulous.*
   D Incorrect. *Crazy* does not have the same meaning as *fabulous.*

5. A **Correct. The word *float* makes sense in both sentences.**
   B Incorrect. The word *tree* does not make sense in either sentence.
   C Incorrect. The word *work* might make sense in the first sentence, but it does not make sense in the second sentence.
   D Incorrect. The word *play* might make sense in the first sentence, but it does not make sense in the second sentence.

Unit 4: Critical Thinking

This unit covers the following critical-thinking skills:

- Author's purpose
- Facts and opinions
- Draw conclusions and make inferences
- Make predictions
- Summarize

Before you begin the unit, have a discussion with students about how people make decisions. Explain that good decision making involves thinking about facts and information. Point out that the skills in this unit will help them make decisions about what they read.

Student page 60 ▶ **Introducing the Unit**

Refer students to the list of critical-thinking skills.

Author's purpose
Facts and opinions
Draw conclusions and make inferences
Make predictions
Summarize

Have students read each skill aloud. To activate prior knowledge, ask students if they know the meaning of each skill.

- Ask *Does anyone know the meaning of author's purpose?* Have volunteers share their responses with the class.
- Ask *Does anyone know the meaning of facts and opinions?* Have volunteers share their responses with the class.
- Ask *Does anyone know the meaning of drawing conclusions and making inferences?* Have volunteers share their responses with the class.
- Ask *Does anyone know the meaning of making predictions?* Have volunteers share their responses with the class.
- Ask *Does anyone know the meaning of summarize?* Have volunteers share their responses with the class.

Reinforce that students will learn about these skills and practice using them. Tell students that at the end of the unit they will have an opportunity to do a personal evaluation of what they have learned. Then ask students to offer examples of each skill. In order to connect learning to their own lives, provide students with additional real-life examples of these skills.
Examples:

Author's purpose: The author wants the reader to believe that dogs make the best pets.

Facts and opinions: Fact: There are more than 340 different kinds of parrots. Opinion: Parrots are the most amazing birds.

Draw conclusions and make inferences: Based on the details in the passage, I think Larry is kind. Based on the details in the passage and what I know, I think Molly is being unfair.

Make predictions: I predict that our baseball team will win the championship.

Summarize: an account of the major events in a television show or sports game

At the End of the Unit

When students finish the skills in this unit, have them return to this page and check the box next to each skill. Then have them complete the exercise at the bottom of the page. In this activity, your students will reflect on the following three things:

- what they learned
- what they feel good about
- what they feel they need more practice with

This exercise makes learning personal and allows students to reflect on what they've learned. Ask students to be active learners. Help them understand that they are responsible for their own learning.

Objective

To use author's purpose to understand the meaning of texts. Students will learn to identify the author's purpose and to answer questions about the author's purpose.

Build Background

Ask students about some of their favorite hobbies or activities. Ask *How did you learn to do these activities? Did you read an article or a book?* Tell the students that we can learn how to do many things by reading "How to" books. When an author writes such a book, he or she has one major purpose in mind: to teach you something. Tell students "How to" books and encyclopedias are examples of writing designed to inform. Ask them to name other types of writing where the author's main purpose is to inform.

Student page 61 ▶ **Learn the Skill**

Discuss with students that knowing the author's purpose will help them know "how" to read a passage and understand what they read.

Coaching Tip

Tell students that the author's purpose can be found by answering the question "Why did the author write this?"

▶ **Apply the Skill**

In this section, students will learn to identify and answer questions about the author's purpose.

- Write on the board *The alligator is America's largest reptile. It can grow to be 19 feet long and weigh 600 pounds. Alligators can live up to 50 years.*
- Have students look at the chart.
- Ask *Why did the author write the passage?* (The author wants to inform the reader about alligators.)
- Have students read the next passage.
- Ask a volunteer to tell what he or she thinks is the author's reason for writing the passage.
- Have students look at the chart on page 61. Ask the volunteer to identify the purpose on the chart that fits the passage. (to persuade)

Student page 62 ▶ **With a Partner**

Have students work together and discuss their thinking with each other and with the class.

- Have pairs of students read the passage.
- Students should discuss the questions after the passage with each other before answering the question about author's purpose.
- Come back together as a class. Discuss students' responses to the questions.
- Ask *What is the author's purpose?* (to persuade)

Think About

Have students review the tools they've learned before beginning the On Your Own activity.

Answers

1. B
2. A
3. D

▶ **On Your Own**

Ask students to work independently on a short practice test.

- Encourage students to ask themselves *Why did the author write this?*
- Come back together as a class and ask students to explain their answer choices. Redirect as necessary.

Differentiated Instruction

Struggling Learners

Cut out short articles from different magazines of interest to the students. Glue the articles to pieces of paper. Distribute the articles to the students and have them match the article to the magazine it came from.

English Language Learners

For students having trouble finding the author's purpose, read an entry or two from an encyclopedia to the students. Ask them to tell you the author's purpose. Repeat the exercise with other sources with very clear purposes, such as a story book, newspaper, or television commercial.

Auditory Learners

Play a song or narrated poem for students. Ask them to find its purpose. (entertain) Ask students to explain what parts of the poem or song helped them find the purpose. (the music, funny words, descriptions of things, tone of voice, etc.)

Your Dictionary

Have students turn to page 252 and write or copy the definition for *author's purpose* and give one example. (author's purpose—the reason or reasons why the author wrote a passage)

Objective

To help students understand that to evaluate different kinds of writing, they must understand the difference between facts and opinions. Using a variety of tools, students will learn to identify facts and opinions in a passage and to answer questions about facts and opinions.

Build Background

Ask	Write
Who has watched a baseball, football, basketball, or soccer game recently?	(list student names)

Ask

What was the final score?	(write the score) *fact*
Did you think the game was exciting?	(write *yes* or *no*) *opinion*

Say *A fact is something that can be proved. An opinion is what someone feels or believes about something. Opinions cannot be proved. Different people may have different opinions about whether the game was exciting or not. However, the score is a fact.*

Student page 64 ▶ **Learn the Skill**

Discuss with students that learning the difference between facts and opinions will help them evaluate all kinds of writing.

Coaching Tip

Tell students that they can often identify opinions by asking themselves if they can prove the statement. For example, they can prove that *October* begins with an *O*, but they can't prove that October is the *best* month of the year.

▶ **Apply the Skill**

In this section, students will learn and use tools to help them identify and answer questions about facts and opinions.

- Write the following on the board. *On July 20, 1969, the first person walked on the moon. I believe it was the most important thing that ever happened in history.*
- Ask *Which of the sentences can be proved?* (On July 20, 1969, the first person walked on the moon.) *How could you prove it?* (Look in an encyclopedia or online.)
- Ask *Which of the sentences tells how someone feels or believes?* (I believe it was the most important thing that ever happened in history.)
- Have students read the next passage and underline the facts and circle the opinions. Draw an empty chart on the board.
- Ask a volunteer whether the first sentence can be proved true. Record the answer as *No* and write *Opinion*. Repeat the procedure for the remaining sentences. Redirect as necessary.
- Have students compare your chart to the one in the book on page 65 to see if they match. Let them know that the chart is a way to organize facts and opinions in a passage. Also tell them they can draw a chart to help them answer questions about facts and opinions.

Student page 65 ▶ **With a Partner**

Answers

Sentence

1: Yes, Fact
2: Yes, Fact
3: Yes, Fact
4: No, Opinion
5: Yes, Fact
6: Yes, Fact
7: No, Opinion
8: No, Opinion

Have students work together and discuss their thinking with each other and with the class.

- Have pairs of students read the passage. Tell them not to fill in the fact and opinion chart in their books yet.
- Come back together as a class. Draw a blank chart on the board.
- Say *I'll read the first sentence.* In the 1800s, many children traveled west in covered wagons. *I think this sentence can be proved true, so I'll write* Yes *in the second column. Because it can be proved, it is a fact. So I'll write* Fact *in the third column.*
- Have students fill in the rest of the fact and opinion chart.
- Invite pairs of students to tell what they wrote in the chart and to explain their thinking. Redirect as necessary. Record the answers in the chart on the board. Continue until all students have recorded the responses for all the sentences.

On Your Own

Ask students to work independently on a short practice test.

- Encourage students to number the sentences in the passage and to draw a fact and opinion chart.
- Come back together as a class and ask students to explain their answer choices. Redirect as necessary.

Student page 66

Think About

Have students review the tools they've learned before beginning the On Your Own activity.

Answers

1. B
2. D
3. C

Differentiated Instruction

Struggling Learners

Challenge students to take turns stating pairs of sentences that contain facts and opinions. Have them explain why each statement is a fact or an opinion. Begin by modeling this example: *It rained on Thursday.* (fact) *Rain makes people feel sad.* (opinion) Have students identify the fact and the opinion. Then have them explain their answer.

English Language Learners

For students having trouble understanding the difference between facts and opinions, bring in pictures such as a landscape. Tape the picture to the board and ask students for a fact (There is a red barn in the picture.) and opinion (The barn is pretty.) about the picture. Then tell students that opinions come from feelings or beliefs about what they see. The color of the barn cannot be disputed, but people might have different opinions about whether or not it is pretty.

Auditory Learners

Have students work in pairs, with one partner playing the role of "Fact" and the other playing the role of "Opinion." Partners role-play by having "Fact" make a statement of fact, such as "We went swimming yesterday." The other partner, "Opinion," should make a statement of opinion about the fact stated by his or her partner, such as "Swimming is fun." Have each pair of students make three such pairs of statements and then switch roles. Have students listening agree or disagree that "Fact" and "Opinion" made accurate statements. Monitor students' statements and redirect where necessary.

Your Dictionary

Have students turn to page 252 and write or copy the definitions for *fact* and *opinion* and give examples. (fact—a statement that can be proved; opinion—what someone feels or believes about something, which cannot be proved)

Objective

To draw conclusions and make inferences to understand text. Students will learn to draw conclusions and make inferences about a passage and to answer questions based on conclusions and inferences.

Build Background

Say *Maria is spreading peanut butter and jelly on bread.* Ask *What do you think she's doing?* (making a peanut butter and jelly sandwich) Ask *How do you know that?* (from the clues *peanut butter, jelly, spreading, bread*) Say *You concluded that from the clues.* Ask *What do you already know about peanut butter and jelly sandwiches?* (They taste good.) *So do you think Maria will like her sandwich or not?* (She will like it.) You inferred that she will like the sandwich because you know that a peanut butter and jelly sandwich tastes good, not from clues in the story.

Student page 67 ▶ ## Learn the Skill

Using details from a passage and what they already know will help students figure out ideas that the author has not directly stated.

Coaching Tip

Point out to students that details about actions and objects can help them draw conclusions or make inferences.

▶ ## Apply the Skill

In this section, students will learn and use tools to help them draw conclusions and make inferences and answer questions about conclusions and inferences.

- Write on the board: *Robert was doing homework when he heard a loud crash. A flash of light lit up the sky. He saw puddles on the ground.*
- Ask *What details in the passage can help you draw a conclusion about what is happening?* (*loud crash, flash of light, puddles*) Underline the details. Say *I underlined the details.*
- Draw an empty chart with the headings *Passage Details* and *Conclusion* on the board. Fill in the details. Say *Thunder is a loud noise, lightning is a flash of light, and rain makes puddles.* Ask *What conclusion can you draw from these details?* (A thunderstorm is taking place.) Fill in the conclusion.
- Have students cover up the chart in the book as they read the next passage and underline details. Draw an empty draw conclusions and make inferences chart on the board.
- Ask a volunteer to tell what he or she underlined and explain his or her thinking. Redirect as necessary. Record details in the chart. Ask a volunteer to tell what he or she knows that can help him or her make an inference. Record the answer.
- Have students compare your chart to the one in the book to see if they match. Let them know that the chart is a way to organize story details and what they know. Tell them they can draw charts to help them answer questions based on conclusions or inferences.

Student page 68 ▶ ## With a Partner

Have students work together and discuss their thinking with each other and with the class.

Answers

Passage Details
drew candles, wrapped a present, picked a flower

What I Know
People make cards and wrap presents for birthdays.

Inference
Alonso is getting ready for a birthday.

Passage Details
Grandmother opened a present, Grandmother cut a cake.

Conclusion
It is Alonso's grandmother's birthday.

- Have pairs of students read the passage. Tell them not to fill in the draw conclusions and make inferences chart in their books yet.
- Come back together as a class.
- Say *I found one passage detail that can help me make an inference about what Alonso is doing.* (Alonso made a card.) *Did you find it? Underline the detail.*
- Draw a chart on the board, fill it in, and have students copy the passage detail in the inference section of their charts.
- Pair students again. Have them look for another detail about what Alonso is doing. Remind students to underline the detail in the passage. Then have them write the detail in their charts. Tell students to use the information in the chart to make an inference.
- Invite pairs to tell what they wrote and to explain their thinking. Redirect as necessary. Record the answers in the chart on the board.
- Tell students to underline passage details that are clues to whose birthday it is. Have students fill in the rest of their charts and draw a conclusion.
- Invite pairs to share what they wrote and explain their thinking.

▶ **On Your Own**

Ask students to work independently on a short practice test.
- Encourage students to underline in the passage and to make a draw conclusions and make inferences chart.
- Come back together as a class and ask students to explain their answer choices. Redirect as necessary.

Think About

Have students review the tools they've learned before beginning the On Your Own activity.

Answers
1. D
2. C
3. A

Differentiated Instruction

Struggling Learners

Ask students to think of something they did for fun recently, either indoors or outdoors. Tell them to think of clues or details that describe what they did. Explain that the clues should not name what they did. Have volunteers take turns telling their clues to the class. Have classmates draw conclusions about what they did. Example: *I put pieces together. I made a picture.* (conclusion: You completed a jigsaw puzzle.)

English Language Learners

For students having trouble drawing conclusions, model story details with pictures that help draw a conclusion about a story. On the board, write *The eggs in the nest had cracks in them. A tiny beak pushed out of one crack.* Read the sentences aloud. Say *Draw pictures to show these sentences.* Then draw a picture to show what was happening. Write *conclusion* under this picture. Ask students to explain their thinking.

Kinesthetic Learners

Have three or more students act out the story. Have one student act out what Sarita does while the other student acts out what the principal does. Have students record the actions in the Passage Details column of the chart. Tell students to fill in what they know about these actions in the What I Know column. Then have students use the information in the chart to make and record an inference.

Your Dictionary

Have students turn to page 252 and write or copy the definitions for *conclusion* and *inference* and give examples. (conclusion—an idea about a given text, based on information from that text; inference—a decision based on prior knowledge plus information in the text)

Objective

To make predictions to better understand texts. Using a variety of tools, students will learn to identify clues in a passage, make predictions, and answer questions about making predictions.

Build Background

Say *Simone forgot her lunch. Isabel, Simone's friend, has two peanut butter sandwiches.* Ask *What do you think happens next?* Write the students' answers on the board. (Isabel gives Simone one of her sandwiches.) Say *When you try to figure out what happens next, you are making a prediction.* Ask *What clues helped you predict that Isabel would give Simone one of her sandwiches?* Write answers on the board. (Answers include: *Simone forgot her lunch. Isabel is Simone's friend. Isabel has an extra sandwich.*)

Student page 70 ▶ **Learn the Skill**

Discuss with students how clues in the passage help to predict what happens.

Coaching Tip

Point out to students that the more information they can find in a passage, the more accurate their prediction will be.

▶ **Apply the Skill**

Students will learn and use tools to help them make predictions.

- Write on the board *The fishing rods stood against the wall in the kitchen. Olga and Kim were excited about the plans for the day.*
- Ask *What will probably happen next?* (Olga and Kim will go fishing.)
- Ask *What clue helped you make that prediction?* Underline *fishing rods, excited,* and *plans.* Say *I underlined the clues.*
- Have students cover the web in their book as they read the next passage and underline the clues. Draw an empty prediction and clues web on the board.
- Ask *What did you predict would happen?*
- In the top circle, write *Vashon will go snowboarding on the hill.*
- Ask *What clues helped you make your prediction?* Fill in the web with *There was snow on the hill. Vashon put on warm clothing. He grabbed his snowboard.*
- Have students compare your web to the one in the book. Tell them that they can draw a web like this to help them answer questions about making predictions and finding clues.

Student page 71 ▶ **With a Partner**

Answers

Clues

1. Rita knows all the plays and rules of the game.
2. The umpire didn't show up.
3. "Maybe we won't have to cancel the game," Ly said.

Prediction

Ly will ask Rita to be the umpire.

Have students work together and discuss their thinking with each other and with the class.

- Have pairs of students read the passage together. Tell them not to fill in the predictions and clues web in their books yet. Encourage them to discuss their thinking with each other.
- Come back together as a class. Draw a blank web on the board.
- Ask *What do you predict will happen?* (Rita will be the umpire for the baseball game.)
- Ask *What were your clues? Underline one clue:* Rita knows all the plays and rules of the game. *Do you see it?*
- Fill in the web on the board with the prediction and one clue. Have students copy the prediction and clue in their web.
- Have students look for other clues in the passage. Remind them to underline the clues in the passage. Ask *What do you think Ly will do next?* (Ask Rita to be the umpire.)
- Invite pairs of students to tell what they wrote in the web and to explain their thinking. Redirect as necessary. Record the answers in the web on the board. Continue until all students have recorded all clues.

▶ **On Your Own**

Ask students to work independently on a short practice test.

- Encourage students to underline in the passage and to draw a prediction and clues web in the margins.
- Come back together as a class and ask students to explain their answer choices. Redirect as necessary.

Think About

Have students review the tools they've learned before beginning the On Your Own activity.

Answers

1. D
2. B
3. B

Differentiated Instruction

Struggling Learners

Ask students to tell you about a prediction they made recently and whether or not it happened. Have students take turns. Examples: *I saw the clouds and knew it was going to rain. I saw my dad put on a warm jacket and get the shovel, and I knew he was going to shovel snow.*

English Language Learners

Ask *What do you think will happen if I ride my bike over a nail?* (The bicycle is going to run over the nail and get a flat tire.) Say *That is a prediction.* Ask *How do you know that is probably going to happen?* (The nail is in the bicycle's path.) *That is your clue about what will probably happen.*

Visual Learners

Pass out simple prompts to students. (examples: a man eats spicy food, a boy throws a ball to a dog, a girl takes an ice cream cone out in the hot sun) Ask students to draw a comic strip depicting their prompt. When students have finished, have them tape a piece of paper over the last panel in the strip. Have students predict what is in the last panel and explain their thinking based on the clues. Reveal the last panel to see if the predictions are correct.

Your Dictionary

Have students turn to page 252 and write or copy the definition for *prediction* and give an example. (prediction—use clues such as titles, pictures, and prior knowledge to guess what a story is about or what will happen next)

Objective

To learn how to identify the information that should be included in a summary. Students will learn to explain the main ideas and most important information in a passage in their own words and answer questions about summarizing.

Build Background

Write *pizza* on the board. Ask students *Who can describe pizza for me?* (possible answer: baked dough covered with sauce and toppings) Write the description in a box on the board. Say *Raise your hand if you like pizza.* Write the students' names under the heading "*Who likes pizza?*" in a box next to the first box. Ask these students *What is one thing you can put on a pizza?* (possible answers: cheese, sausage, mushrooms) Write the ingredients on the board under the heading "*What can you put on a pizza?*" in a third box next to the second box. Explain that you have made a summary web showing two main ideas about pizza that can go into a summary. Say *The main idea of our discussion is pizza, which is baked dough covered with toppings. To make a summary, we want to include all of the main ideas, but in our own words with only the most important details.* Guide the students in writing a summary of the discussion. (possible summary: Pizza is baked dough covered with sauce and toppings such as cheese and sausage. It is popular with our class.) Point out that not every detail was included, but the main ideas and answers to *what, who,* and *how* were answered in the summary.

Student page 73 ▶ **Learn the Skill**

Discuss with students how to summarize to make sure they understand it.

Apply the Skill

In this section, students will learn and use tools to help them summarize.

Coaching Tip

The main idea is usually found near the beginning of a passage, but sometimes it can be near the end.

- Write *Lamar's cat is afraid of thunderstorms. He hates to get wet when it rains. Every time there is thunder and lightning, Lamar's cat hides under the bed. He doesn't come out until the storm is over.*
- Ask *What is this passage about?* (Lamar's cat is afraid of thunderstorms and doesn't come out until the storm is over.) Circle the words that show the main ideas. Say *I circled the main ideas.*
- Ask *What's a summary of this passage?* (Lamar's cat is afraid of storms. He hides under the bed until the storm is over.)
- Have students cover the web in their book as they read the next passage and circle the main ideas. Draw an empty web on the board.
- Ask a volunteer to tell what he or she circled and to explain his or her thinking. Write the answer in the web on the board. Redirect as necessary.
- Have students compare your web to the one in the book. Tell them that the summary web is a good way to find the main ideas in a passage.

Student page 74 ▶ **With a Partner**
Answers

Main Ideas:
Omar could see better with his new glasses.
Omar's grades began to improve.
His glasses helped him play baseball better.

Summary:
Omar could see better with his new glasses. His grades improved because he could see the board. He also played baseball better.

Have students work together and discuss their thinking with each other and with the class.

- Have pairs of students read the passage.
- Draw a blank summary web on the board.
- Ask a volunteer to state a main idea. (Omar could see better with his new glasses.) Circle it and write the answer in the web. Invite students to write it in their web in their book.
- Say *I found another main idea.* (Omar's grades began to improve.) *Do you see it? Circle it.*
- Have students add a third main idea to the web in their books. (His glasses helped him play baseball better.)
- Invite student pairs to the board to draw their summary webs and explain their thinking. Redirect as necessary.
- Have students write a summary of the passage and share it with the class. Have students take turns.

▶ **On Your Own**

Ask students to work independently on a short practice test.
- Encourage students to circle the main ideas in the passage and to draw a summary web.
- Come back together as a class and ask students to explain their answer choices. Redirect as necessary.

Student page 75

Think About

Have students review circling the main ideas and drawing summary webs before they begin the On Your Own activity.

Answers
1. D
2. C

Differentiated Instruction

Struggling Learners

Ask students to tell you about a story they read or a movie they watched recently, perhaps as a class project or activity. Draw a summary web on the board. Ask them to explain it.

English Language Learners

Give students a topic sentence and have them provide main ideas. For example, say *When you are thirsty, you have many choices.* Ask them what the choices include. Have them write the main ideas and any important details in a summary web. Then have them write a summary using information in the web.

Auditory Learners

Have students read the passages out loud to each other instead of silently, then circle and fill in the summary webs.

Your Dictionary

Have students turn to page 252 and write or copy the definition for *summary* and give an example. (summary—explains the most important parts of a passage in fewer words, including all of the main ideas.)

Answers

The Family Dinner

1. A Incorrect. This is a fact that is stated in the passage.
   B **Correct. This is an opinion that cannot be proved true or false.**
   C Incorrect. This is a fact that is stated in the passage.
   D Incorrect. This is a fact that is stated in the passage.

2. A Incorrect. The passage indicates that the family often has dinner together.
   B Incorrect. There is nothing in the passage to suggest that they watch television together.
   C Incorrect. There is nothing in the passage to suggest that they have boring talks.
   D **Correct. The passage indicates that the family talks and gets along well.**

3. A Incorrect. While he *may* leave the table, it is not the thing that is *most likely* to happen next.
   B **Correct. There have been many jokes so far, so it is likely there will be another one soon.**
   C Incorrect. The passage gives no indication that this will happen.
   D Incorrect. There is nothing in the passage to suggest that this will happen next

4. A **Correct. The author has included many jokes in the passage.**
   B Incorrect. Italy is mentioned, but the purpose of the passage is more to entertain than to persuade.
   C Incorrect. The passage mentions pasta but does not tell much about it.
   D Incorrect. The passage does not suggest anything about healthy eating habits.

5. A Incorrect. This answer does not include the most important parts of the passage. It does not include the main ideas.
   B Incorrect. This answer does not include the most important parts of the passage. It does not include the main ideas.
   C **Correct. This answer includes the most important parts of the passage and the main ideas.**
   D Incorrect. This answer does not include the most important parts of the passage. It does not include the main ideas.

6. A **Correct. His smile was in response to the joke she made.**
   B Incorrect. The father made no mention of her school situation.
   C Incorrect. There are no clues in the passage that suggest he's glad she likes pasta.
   D Incorrect. The passage does not indicate that she knows how to cook.

Answers

The Old Oak Tree

1. A Incorrect. All the details in the passage are not about the building of the tree house.
   B Incorrect. The description of picnics is a detail, not the main idea.
   C **Correct. All of the details are about getting a tree house in their favorite tree.**
   D Incorrect. The cookies are a detail, not the main idea.

2. A Incorrect. Unsuccessful does not mean "full of ideas."
   B Incorrect. The meaning of *unsuccessful* is not "like a tired person."
   C **Correct. Elsa and Oscar are afraid they will not achieve their goal, which is to persuade Mama to climb up to the tree house.**
   D Incorrect. *Unsuccessful* is not necessarily related to "not trying."

3. A **Correct. This is the correct order of events.**
   B Incorrect. First they made a plan. Then they made a list.
   C Incorrect. They went to the store last. First they made a plan and then a list.
   D Incorrect. After they made a plan, they made a list, and then went to the store.

4. A Incorrect. The passage does not mention a park.
   B Incorrect. The passage does not mention sand or water, which you would find at a beach.
   C **Correct. The setting of the passage is in the tree house, where they have a picnic.**
   D Incorrect. Only a small part of the passage mentions the store.

5. A Incorrect. Elsa does not jump down. Oscar has to talk her down.
   B **Correct. Elsa *does* get stuck in the tree.**
   C Incorrect. Mama does not yell at Elsa.
   D Incorrect. Elsa likes to read in the tree. Oscar likes to draw pictures.

6. A Incorrect. Oscar likes to draw up in the tree.
   B Incorrect. Elsa likes to read up in the tree.
   C **Correct. Both Elsa and Oscar like climbing the tree.**
   D Incorrect. Only Elsa has been stuck in the tree.

7. A Incorrect. Oscar is not selfish. He likes to help others.
   B Incorrect. Oscar is kind and helpful to others.
   C Incorrect. Oscar is happy but does not try to make others laugh.
   D **Correct. Oscar is very helpful to Elsa and helps Papa build a tree house.**

Animals Among Us

8. A Incorrect. *Why We Should Respect Them* would describe how people should act around chipmunks and squirrels.
   B Incorrect. *Where They Live* would tell about their homes, not their food.
   C **Correct. *What They Eat* would tell what chipmunks eat.**
   D Incorrect. *What Hunts Them* would tell which animals hunt chipmunks.

9. A Incorrect. *Brush* in paragraph 1 is where the animals live; it is not a hairbrush.
   B **Correct. The animals live in *brush*, a place with small trees and bushes.**
   C Incorrect. *Brush* in paragraph 1 tells where animals live.
   D Incorrect. *Brush* in paragraph 1 tells where animals live.

10. A **Correct. Every paragraph tells how chipmunks and squirrels are alike or different.**
    B Incorrect. The passage tells only about chipmunks and squirrels.
    C Incorrect. The author does not tell how to keep chipmunks out of houses.
    D Incorrect. The author does not tell how to feed squirrels in the wild.

11. A **Correct. The passage gives information about chipmunks and squirrels.**
    B Incorrect. This passage is serious and gives facts.
    C Incorrect. This passage does not tell how to do or make something or how to get from one place to another.
    D Incorrect. This passage does not try to convince readers of something.

12. A Incorrect. This is incorrect information; thus, the sentence does not complete the summary.
    B Incorrect. This is incorrect; thus, the sentence does not complete the summary.
    C **Correct. This sentence about how to treat chipmunks and squirrels completes the summary of the passage.**
    D Incorrect. This is incorrect; thus, the sentence does not complete the summary.

13. A Incorrect. *Chubby* does not mean "dark."
    B **Correct. *Chubby* means that the faces look fat.**
    C Incorrect. *Chubby* does not mean "lumpy."
    D Incorrect. *Chubby* does not mean "little."

14. A Incorrect. Only the tree squirrel is shown with strong legs.
    B **Correct. The diagrams show that both animals have claws and big eyes.**
    C Incorrect. The tree squirrel has a bushy tail, and the chipmunk has a furry tail.
    D Incorrect. The diagrams don't show anything about food.

Whoooo's There

15. A Incorrect. *Brilliant* does not mean "dull"; a dull moon would not light up a yard.
    B **Correct. A "bright" moon would light up a yard.**
    C Incorrect. *Brilliant* does not mean "yellow." A "yellow" moon might not light up a yard.
    D Incorrect. *Brilliant* does not mean "far away"; a "far away" moon wouldn't light up a yard.

16. A Incorrect. This is a fact that can be proved, not an opinion.
    B Incorrect. This is a fact that can be proved, not an opinion.
    C Incorrect. Both girls heard the owl hoot. This is stated as a fact.
    D **Correct. This is not a fact that can be proved.**

17. A Incorrect. No mention is made of either girl trusting someone.
    B **Correct. The passage is about two girls and a wild owl in its natural environment.**
    C Incorrect. It is not about honesty or what the girls learn about honesty.
    D Incorrect. The characters are good, but they do not face anything evil.

18. A Incorrect. No mention is made of Sharice reading.
    B **Correct. The entire passage is about Sharice watching a great horned owl.**
    C Incorrect. Sharice is glad for the light of the moon.
    D Incorrect. The passage says it was cold; it does not say Sharice likes cold weather.

19. A Incorrect. Sharice states that they will look for the owl on the next night.
    B Incorrect. Sharice wants to look for the owl, not play a game.
    C Incorrect. Nothing is said about Tamia eating dinner.
    D **Correct. *Tamia yawned and walked toward her bedroom* indicates she will go to bed.**

20. A **Correct. Both buttons and an owl's eyes are round.**
    B Incorrect. An owl's eyes are not made of plastic.
    C Incorrect. Buttons are not found in nature.
    D Incorrect. Buttons are not always yellow.

Before You Begin

Step 2 is the second step in the three-step approach and covers pages 85–168 in the student book. Instruction is at an intermediate level to ensure that students have a solid foundation in the vocabulary.

To meet the needs of struggling learners and English language learners, the readability is approximately one grade below level, passages are medium length (half a page), and reading material is high interest. This helps students develop fluency by allowing them to focus on the vocabulary being taught with little distraction from the language.

Step 2 presents vocabulary strategies at the most foundational level, graphic organizers that are uncomplicated, and short practice passages that help students practice the strategy. This attention to vocabulary will help students become successful and more confident readers. Use the Student Skill Progress Chart on pages 116–117 to track each student's progress on the skills. The Skills and Items Correlation on page 118 will help you identify which questions in the unit and step reviews test each skill.

Introduction to Step 2

The Introduction to Step 2 reviews skills learned in Step 1 and focuses on vocabulary and strategies students will use throughout the step. Ensuring that students are comfortable with these concepts before they begin skill instruction on page 90 in the student book will allow them to focus on understanding the vocabulary. Tell students that they will learn tools and vocabulary that will help them manage the information they read and become better readers.

Student page 86 ▶ **About Questions First**

Students will learn the strategy of reading the questions before reading the passage. Explain to students that this is an important strategy because it will help them know what to look for in passages and alert them to any important vocabulary being used.

- Ask a volunteer to read the explanation of Questions First. Then use the bulleted list to explain how to read questions first.
- Have pairs of students read the example passage and question. Then have them answer the question together.
- Regroup as a class and have students share their answers. (1. B) Redirect as necessary.

About Special Treatment of Words

Students will learn how words can be written in special ways. Introduce students to the concepts of capital letters and boldface.

- Write the following on the board: *Which flavors of ice cream do students in your class like BEST?*
- Ask students to identify the word with special treatment.
- Repeat with an example of a boldfaced word.
- Then ask pairs of students to read the next question and identify the word with special treatment. Have students read the passage and answer the question.
- Regroup as a class and have students share their answers. (1. C) Redirect as necessary.

About the Check Back Box

The Check Back feature is one of three that students will become familiar with throughout the book at point of use. It directs students to specific pages where tools they've already learned are presented. The Check Back box appears in Steps 2 and 3.

Check Back Box

- Direct students to the Check Back box and explain that it shows them a page number where a tool they've already learned was presented.
- Have a volunteer flip back to page 5 to find examples of tools they can use.
- Ask the class to discuss why the Check Back box was included in this section.

Student page 87 ▶ ### About Question Words

Students will learn words that are common in questions throughout the book. These words may be unfamiliar to students, so careful explanation and examples are needed to help them understand.

- Ask a volunteer to read the definition of *According to*. Then explain that in most questions, *according to* will mean "in" when it refers to a paragraph or passage and "in the opinion of" when it refers to a person.
- Offer real-life examples, such as: *According to this fire safety map, we are supposed to exit the classroom door and turn left if there is a fire. According to my mother, I was the noisiest baby in the world.*
- Repeat the process for *Which of these* and *Which of the following.*
- Have pairs of students reread the passage and answer Questions 2 and 3.
- Regroup as a class and have students share their answers. (2. D 3. B) Redirect as necessary.

Student page 88 ▶ ### About Signal Words

Students will learn that signal words are words that give clues to what they read. They will also learn to draw boxes around signal words.

- Ask a volunteer to read the definition of *signal words.* Then list examples on the board, such as *words that signal danger: watch out, warning, emergency.*
- Invite the class to list more words that signal danger.
- Have students read the example sentence that includes the boxed signal word *before.* Discuss its meaning within the sentence.
- As a class, read the passage aloud. Encourage students to raise their hands when they hear a word that signals when something happens.
- Pause when students raise their hands to discuss whether the word is a signal word and draw a box around the word if it is.

About the Tip Box

Direct students to the Tip box and explain that it gives them a hint to help them answer questions. The Tip box appears in Step 2.

About Words to Watch Out For

Students will learn the words *except* and *not.* These words can be confusing because they change what is being discussed or asked.

- Read the explanation for *except* and *not* aloud to students.
- Have volunteers read the passage and answer Question 1.
- Regroup as a class and discuss the tricky word (*not*) and how it changes the meaning of the question. Have students share their answers. (1. C) Redirect as necessary.

Unit 1: Comprehension

Student page 89

Main idea and
   supporting
   details
Sequence
Compare and
   contrast
Cause and effect

▶ Introducing the Unit

Have students refer back to the list of comprehension skills found on page 7 of Unit 1. Have students read each skill aloud. To activate prior knowledge, ask students if they remember the meaning of each skill.

- Say *I am going to read a short passage. Listen closely to the words.*
     Mark is always part of a school sports team. He plays football, soccer, baseball, and basketball. More than anything else, Mark loves playing baseball.
  Ask *What is the main idea of the passage?* Have volunteers share their responses with the class.
- Ask *What does sequence mean? What are some words that tell you about sequence?* Have volunteers share their responses with the class.
- Say *Listen carefully to this passage.*
     Both backpacks are large and strong. The red backpack, however, is lighter than the blue one.
  Ask *How would you compare the two backpacks? How would you contrast the two backpacks?* Have volunteers share their responses with the class.
- Say *I am going to read a short passage. Listen closely to the words.*
     Lee and Juan were walking to school. They saw an injured bird and stopped to look at it. Juan wanted to take it home, but Lee said that was a bad idea. Because the boys talked about the bird for so long, they were late to school.
- Ask *What caused Lee and Juan to be late for school?* Have volunteers share their responses with the class.

Remind students that they will continue to learn how to use these skills. Then explain that at the end of the unit they will have an opportunity to do a personal evaluation of what they learned.

Examples:

Main idea: A woman starts her own business.

Sequence: following the instructions for how to build a model; washing dishes in the correct order

Compare and contrast: explaining how two dogs are similar or different; describing the differences between you and your cousin

Cause and effect: catching a cold, missing school, and then not being able to go out and play because you have extra homework to make up

At the End of the Unit

When students finish the skills in this unit, have them return to this page and complete the exercise at the bottom. In this activity, your students will reflect on the following three things:

- what they learned
- what they feel good about
- what they feel they need more practice with

This exercise makes learning personal and allows students to reflect on what they've learned. Ask students to be active learners. Help them understand that they are responsible for their own learning.

Objective

To use signal words to identify the main idea and supporting details in a passage.

Student page 90

Coaching Tip

Tell students that sometimes the author tells the main idea in the first sentence, and other times it is at the end of the passage.

Check Back

Tell students to turn to page 9 to remember what a main idea web looks like.

▶ **Review the Skill**

Review how to identify the main idea and supporting details and the tools students have learned. Remind them that the main idea tells what a passage is about. Give examples and ask students to identify the main ideas and supporting details.

Learn the Vocabulary

Students learn about signal words that help them identify main idea questions.

- Have students read the passage and question 1 that follows. Direct students' attention to the word *mostly* in the question. Tell them that the word is a main idea signal word.
- Then have students identify the supporting details that tell about the main idea. (*opened a lemonade stand, mowed neighbors' lawns, watered their flowers*)
- Invite them to explain how they knew what to underline and circle.

▶ **Apply the Vocabulary**

Have students find the signal words in question 2.

- Ask students to draw a box around the signal words in the question. (*most of all*)
- Invite students to draw a completed main idea web on the board and explain their thinking to the class. Redirect as necessary.

Signal Words	
the best	detail
main idea	most important
most of all	mostly

Student page 91

Tip

Remind students that words such as *mostly* signal that a question is asking for a main idea.

▶ **With a Partner**

Have students work together through a short passage.

- Draw attention to the boldfaced instructions and ask a volunteer to read them aloud.
- Point out to students that one question is below the passage and the other four are on the next page. Have them draw a box around the signal words in the question. (1. *mostly*)
- Have pairs of students read the passage and answer only the first question together. (1. D)

Student page 92

Think About

Have students review the tools they've learned before beginning the On Your Own activity.

▶ **On Your Own**

Have students work independently to answer more questions about the same passage.

- After students answer the questions, regroup as a class and ask students which words signaled important details and the main idea. (signal words: 2. *mostly* 3. *main idea*)
- Have them explain their answer choices. (2. B 3. C 4. A 5. C) Redirect as necessary.

> **English Language Learners**
>
> Have students listen to a story that names several important details. Then have them tell the main idea. For example, *My dog is getting old. She does not run for the ball anymore. She does not like to go up and down the stairs. She sleeps a lot during the day. My dog is almost 11 years old.*

Step 2 Skill 2 ■ Sequence

Objective
To use sequence signal words to identify sequence questions and to find sequence in passages.

Student page 93 ▶ **Review the Skill**
Review how to identify steps or events and the tools students have learned. Remind them that sequence is the order in which events occur. Give examples and ask students to identify the steps in sequence. Then ask them to share a story or process that tells events in order.

Coaching Tip

Point out to students that words that tell about time help readers understand the sequence of events in a passage.

Learn the Vocabulary
Students learn about signal words that help them identify sequence.
- Have a student read the first sentence in the passage. Direct students' attention to *this morning*. Tell them that *this morning* signals sequence.
- Then have students identify and number the next two events. (*They both hid* and *the sun came out.*)
- Invite them to explain how they knew what to number.

▶ **Apply the Vocabulary**
Have students find signal words and draw a box around each one.

Check Back

Tell students to turn to page 12 to remember what a step chart looks like.

- Ask students to identify and draw a box around the other signal words in the passage. (*this afternoon* and *this evening*) Ask students to identify the event that *this afternoon* signals and have them draw and fill in a chart in their books.

Signal Words		
first	yesterday	this morning
second	today	this afternoon
third	tomorrow	this evening
next	before	now
then	after	later
finally		

- Invite students to draw a completed step chart on the board and explain their thinking to the class. Redirect as necessary.

Student page 94 ▶ **With a Partner**
Have students work together and discuss their thinking while working through a short passage.
- Draw attention to the boldfaced instructions and ask a volunteer to read them aloud.
- Point out to students that one question is below the passage and the other four are on the next page. Have them draw a box around the signal words in the first question. (1. *first*)
- Have pairs of students read the passage and answer only the first question. (1. B)
- Have volunteers share which signal words they found in the passage (paragraph 2: *before, after* paragraph 3: *after* paragraph 4: *first, then, next, finally*) and explain their thinking. Redirect as necessary.

Tip

Tell students that when they see *when* in a question, they need to look for the sequence in the passage.

Student page 95 ▶ **On Your Own**
Have students work independently to answer more questions about the same passage.
- After students answer the questions, regroup as a class and ask students which words signaled sequence. (2. *after* 3. *before* 4. *before* 5. *last*)
- Then have them explain their answer choices. (2. D 3. C 4. B 5. A) Redirect as necessary.

Think About

Have students review the tools they have learned before beginning the On Your Own activity.

English Language Learners

Have students listen to short retellings of stories that include no more than three events. Then have them retell or act out the story in correct sequence. Example: *This morning it snowed. Then this afternoon the sun came out. By the evening, the snow had melted.*

Objective
To use compare and contrast signal words to identify compare and contrast relationships and to find the relationships in passages.

Student page 96 ▶ **Review the Skill**
Remind students that when you compare, you look for ways in which two things are alike. When you contrast, you look for ways in which two things are different. Give examples and ask students to identify compare and contrast. Example: *Yesterday and today were both sunny days, but yesterday was colder than today.*

Coaching Tip

Tell students that *both* and *but* are two common signal words for compare and contrast.

▶ **Learn the Vocabulary**
Students learn about signal words that identify compare and contrast.
- Have a student read the first sentence in the passage. Direct students' attention to *as well as* and *Both*. Tell them that *as well as* and *Both* signal a comparison.
- Have students identify and circle how pens and pencils are similar in the first paragraph.

Check Back

Tell students to turn to page 14 to recall what a compare and contrast diagram looks like.

▶ **Apply the Vocabulary**
Have students find signal words and draw a box around each one.
- Ask students to read the rest of the passage and draw a box around the signal words. (*while, however*) Have students draw and fill in a compare and contrast diagram.
- Invite students to share their answers and to explain their thinking. Redirect as necessary.

Signal Words for Comparing		
alike	also	as well as
both	just like	same as
similar	too	in the same way
Signal Words for Contrasting		
although	but	different
however	though	unlike
on the other hand	while	

Student page 97 ▶ **With a Partner**
Have students work together through a short passage.

Tip

Point out to students that the word *both* tells you that two things are similar.

- Draw attention to the boldfaced instructions and ask a volunteer to read them aloud.
- Point out to students that one question is below the passage and the other four are on the next page. Have them draw a box around all signal words found in the first question. (1. *similar*)
- Have pairs of students read the passage and answer only the first question. (1. C)
- Have volunteers share which signal words they found in the passage. (paragraph 1: *both, but, while* paragraph 2: *on the other hand, both, although* paragraph 3: *also, however, while* paragraph 4: *in the same way, too* paragraph 5: *though, both, while*) Redirect as necessary.

Student page 98 ▶ **On Your Own**
Have students work independently to answer more questions about the same passage.
- After students answer the questions, regroup as a class and ask students which words signaled compare and contrast. (signal words: 2. *though, both* 3. *different* 4. *both, but*) Have them explain their answer choices. (2. A 3. B 4. B 5. C) Redirect as necessary.

Think About

Have students review the tools they have learned before beginning the On Your Own activity.

English Language Learners

Review words in the passage with which students may not be familiar, such as *California, Florida, West Coast, East Coast, Atlantic Ocean, Pacific Ocean,* and *surfing.* Show them where these states, regions, and oceans are on a map. Show them a picture of someone surfing. Have them either complete or write sentences using these terms.

Objective

To use cause and effect signal words to identify cause and effect questions and to find the relationships in passages.

Student page 99 ▶ **Review the Skill**

Review how to find cause and effect and the tools students have learned. Remind them that the cause is why something happens. The effect is what happened because of the cause. Give examples and ask students to identify cause and effect. For example: *I stubbed my toe* (effect) *because I tripped over my cat* (cause).

▶ **Learn the Vocabulary**

Coaching Tip

Tell students that the words that come <u>after</u> *because* give a reason why something happened.

Students learn about signal words that identify cause and effect.

- Have a student read the first sentence in the passage. Direct students' attention to *because*. Tell them that *because* is a signal word that shows cause and effect.
- Then have students identify and circle the cause and identify and underline the effect. (cause: *She was the star of the school play*; effect: *Alita was excited.*)
- Invite them to explain how they knew what to underline and circle.

▶ **Apply the Vocabulary**

Check Back

Tell students to turn to page 17 to remember what a cause and effect chart looks like.

Have students find signal words and draw a box around each one.

- Ask students to draw a box around the signal words in the last sentence of the passage. (*so that*) Ask students to identify the cause and effect and have them draw and fill in a chart.
- Invite students to share their answers and to explain their thinking to the class. Redirect as necessary.

Signal Words	
as a result	because
cause	reason
since	so
so that	therefore
why	

Student page 100 ▶ **With a Partner**

Tip

Point out to students that when they see *why* in a question, they need to look for a cause in the passage.

Have students work together through a short passage.

- Draw attention to the boldfaced instructions and ask a volunteer to read them aloud.
- Point out to students that one question is below the passage and the other four are on the next page. Have them draw a box around the signal word in the first question. (1. *Why*)
- Have pairs of students read the passage and answer only the first question. (1. A)
- Have volunteers share which signal words they found in the passage (paragraph 1: *because, because* paragraph 2: *why, cause* paragraph 3: *because, so* paragraph 4: *since*) and explain their thinking. Redirect as necessary.

Student page 101 ▶ **On Your Own**

Think About

Have students review the tools they've learned before beginning the On Your Own activity.

Have students work independently to answer more questions about the same passage.

- After students answer the questions, regroup as a class and ask students which words signaled cause and effect. (signal words: 2. *reason* 3. *because* 4. *because* 5. *why*) Have them explain their answer choices. (2. C 3. A 4. A 5. D) Redirect as necessary.

English Language Learners

Have students finish sentence frames using a signal word for cause and effect. For example, *It's raining today. . . (so I can't play outside). I lost my gloves. . . (so my hands got cold). I wish I could eat pizza every day. . . (because it's my favorite food).*

Answers

Take Cover!

1. A   Incorrect. Only earthquakes cause the earth to shake.
   B   Incorrect. Hurricanes do not happen suddenly. This is a difference between the two.
   C   Correct. Both can cause a lot of damage.
   D   Incorrect. Only hurricanes form over the ocean. This is a difference between the two.

2. A   Incorrect. Hurricanes do not cause the earth to shake, earthquakes do.
   B   Correct. Hurricanes can cause big waves.
   C   Incorrect. The earth does not release energy during a hurricane.
   D   Incorrect. Fault lines relate to earthquakes.

3. A   Incorrect. This is the wind speed of hurricanes and does not explain earthquakes in California.
   B   Incorrect. There are rocks beneath the surface of the earth, but the passage does not list this as a specific cause of earthquakes in southern California.
   C   Correct. Paragraph 3 states that because of a large fault line in southern California, there are nearly ten thousand earthquakes each year.
   D   Incorrect. Warm water can be a cause of hurricanes, but this fact does not explain why there are earthquakes in southern California.

4. **A   Correct. This is the first thing mentioned in paragraph 7.**
   B   Incorrect. This is the last thing to do.
   C   Incorrect. This is the second thing to do.
   D   Incorrect. This is not the first thing to do.

5. A   Incorrect. This has nothing to do with preparation.
   B   Correct. According to paragraph 8, this is something important to do.
   C   Incorrect. This is something you would do after a hurricane has come.
   D   Incorrect. According to paragraph 8, you should do this *after* a hurricane.

6. A   Incorrect. Both are serious natural events.
   B   Incorrect. Both can cause serious damage.
   C   Correct. Only hurricanes form over ocean water.
   D   Incorrect. Both happen in the United States.

7. A   Incorrect. Stored energy in the earth relates to earthquakes, not hurricanes.
   B   Incorrect. Hurricanes are not mentioned as causing problems in California, and earthquakes are not mentioned as events in Texas, Florida, and the Gulf Coast.
   C   Correct. The first, sixth, and last paragraphs mention that we must know what to do if these events happen, and specific preparations are suggested in paragraphs 7 and 8.
   D   Incorrect. Listening to local radio and television is mentioned as something important to do after a hurricane, but it is not the main idea of the passage.

Unit 2: Fiction and Nonfiction Skills

Student page 104 ▶ **Introducing the Unit**

Character
Plot and setting
Theme
Literary elements
Structural elements
Visual information
Nonfiction writing

Have students refer back to the list of fiction and nonfiction skills found on page 22 of Unit 2. Have students read each skill aloud. To activate prior knowledge, ask students if they remember the meaning of each skill.

- Say *I am going to read a short passage. Listen closely.*
  Karl helps his mom clean the house. He washes the car for his father. He also helps his little brother with his homework.
- Ask *What does this passage tell you about Karl's character?* Have volunteers share their responses with the class.
- Ask *What is the setting of a story you have read?* Have volunteers share their responses with the class.
- Ask *What is the theme of a story you have read?* Have volunteers share their responses with the class.
- Ask *What is an example of a simile or a metaphor?* Have volunteers share their responses with the class.
- Say *Name two structural elements you might find in a nonfiction book.* Have volunteers share their responses with the class.
- Ask *What kinds of visual information have you seen in a book or article?* Have volunteers share their responses with the class.
- Ask *What are some examples of nonfiction writing you have read?* Have volunteers share their responses with the class.

Reinforce that students will learn about these skills and practice using them. Tell students that at the end of the unit they will have an opportunity to do a personal evaluation of what they have learned.

Examples:

Character: Donna practiced for the race for over a year. Donna is strong and determined.

Plot and setting: On a small farm in the country, Pierre spends the summer with his cousins and does lots of fun things.

Theme: Jenna learned that difficult tasks can be completed if you work hard.

Literary elements: The field was as flat as a pancake.

Structural elements: a heading, a subheading, a title

Visual information: a chart showing how many goals each person on the team scored

Nonfiction writing: a biography of Helen Keller

At the End of the Unit

When students finish the skills in this unit, have them return to this page and complete the exercise at the bottom. In this activity, your students will reflect on the following three things:

- what they learned
- what they feel good about
- what they feel they need more practice with

This exercise makes learning personal and allows students to reflect on what they've learned. Ask students to be active learners. Help them understand that they are responsible for their own learning.

Objective

To use character signal words to identify character questions.

Student page 105 ▶ **Review the Skill**

Review how to find character clues and the tools students have learned. Remind students to look for what the character says and does and then ask what kind of person says and does those things.

▶ **Learn the Vocabulary**

Students learn about signal words that help them look for questions about characters.

- Have a student read aloud the question following the passage. Direct students' attention to *feel*. Tell them that *feel* signals that the question is asking for information about Dmitri's feelings.
- Have students identify and underline the words Dmitri says and identify and circle his actions. (words: *I feel like a real cowboy!*, *I'm not riding that thing!*, and *I only wanted to* play *cowboy!* actions: jumping behind the speaker)
- Invite them to explain how they knew what to underline and circle.

Signal Words
character
emotion
kind of person
think
feel
act
behave

Coaching Tip

To find clues about the character, direct students to look for sentences that mention the character's name.

▶ **Apply the Vocabulary**

Have students find signal words and draw a box around each one.

- Ask students to identify the signal word in the question. (*kind of person*) Ask them what they know about the character from the passage. (He is playful.)
- Have them draw and fill in the character clues web.
- Invite students to share their answers and to explain their thinking to the class. Redirect as necessary.

Check Back

Tell students to turn to page 23 to remember what a character clues web looks like.

Student page 106 ▶ **With a Partner**

Have students work together through a short passage.

- Draw attention to the boldfaced instructions and ask a volunteer to read them aloud.
- Point out to students that one question is below the passage and the other four are on the next page. Have them draw a box around the signal word in the first question. (1. *behave*)
- Have pairs of students read the passage and answer only the first question together. (1. B)

Tip

Point out to students that a character's words often tell you how the character thinks and feels.

Student page 107 ▶ **On Your Own**

Have students work independently to answer more questions about the same passage.

- After students answer the questions, regroup as a class and ask students which words signaled character. (signal words: 2. *kind of person* 3. *feel* 5. *cares*)
- Then have them explain their answer choices. (2. B 3. D 4. A 5. C) Redirect as necessary.

Think About

Have students review the tools they've learned before beginning the On Your Own activity.

English Language Learners

Have students finish sentence frames to get a feeling for character traits. Examples: *My grandmother feels that . . .* or *I think that friends should always . . .* or *She acts like she does not . . . .*

Objective
To use plot and setting signal words to identify plot and setting questions.

Student page 108 ▶ **Review the Skill**
Review how to find plot and setting and the tools students have learned. Say *The plot is the actions and events in a story. Where and when the story takes place are the setting.*

Coaching Tip

Point out that there are many words that can signal plot and setting. The words in the box are only a few possibilities.

▶ **Learn the Vocabulary**
In this section, students learn about signal words that help them identify plot and setting.
- Have a student read aloud the question following the passage. Direct students' attention to the word *problem*. Tell them that *problem* signals an event in the plot of the passage.
- Then have students identify and underline the action words (*did not know, stared, decided to do his homework, thought*) and circle the words that relate to setting (*room, supper would not be ready for another hour*).
- Invite them to explain how they knew what to underline and circle.

Signal Words for Plot
happens
occurs
takes place
problem
solve
plot
Signal Words for Setting
where
when
place
time
location
setting

Check Back

Tell students to turn to page 26 to remember what a plot and setting chart looks like.

▶ **Apply the Vocabulary**
Have students draw a box around the signal words.
- Have students draw a box around the plot signal word in the question.
- Invite students to draw a completed plot and setting chart on the board and explain their thinking to the class. Redirect as necessary.

Student page 109 ▶ **With a Partner**
Have students work together through a short passage.
- Draw attention to the boldfaced instructions and ask a volunteer to read them aloud.
- Point out to students that one question is below the passage and the other four are on the next page. Have them draw a box around the signal word in the first question. (1. *where*)
- Have pairs of students read the passage and answer only the first question. (1. C)

Tip

Tell students to look for clues that tell them what is happening and when and where a passage takes place.

Student page 110 ▶ **On Your Own**
Have students work independently to answer more questions about the same passage.
- After students answer the questions, regroup as a class and ask students which words signaled plot and setting. (signal words: *2. when 3. setting 4. problem 5. setting*) Have them explain their answer choices. (2. A 3. A 4. C 5. B) Redirect as necessary.

Think About

Have students review the tools they've learned before beginning the On Your Own activity.

English Language Learners

Have students tell about events that have happened to them to get a feeling for plot and setting. Have them begin by finishing the following sentence: *I remember when . . . .*

Objective
To learn vocabulary of themes often found in stories.

Student page 111 ▶ **Review the Skill**

Review how to find the theme and the tools students have learned.
Say *The theme is a message about life.* Ask *What are some movies or TV shows that you have seen recently?* Write the responses on the board. Ask *What lesson did the characters learn or how did the characters change? What theme was suggested?* Write students' responses in a theme chart on the board.

Coaching Tip

Explain to students that not all themes are found on the list. These are just some of the most common themes in stories.

▶ **Learn the Vocabulary**

In this section, students learn about words that describe common themes in passages.
- Present the common themes. Discuss their meanings with the class.
- Have a student read the passage aloud.
- Then have students identify how Dan changes or the lesson Dan learns.
- Invite students to explain where they see this lesson in the passage.

Common Themes

Personal Growth: bravery, following rules, understanding responsibility, working hard, honesty
Friendship: trusting others, forgiving others, supporting others, being in a group is better than being alone
Common Struggles: good wins over evil, love is stronger than hate, honesty is better than lying

---

Check Back

Tell students to turn to page 29 to remember what a theme chart looks like.

▶ **Apply the Vocabulary**

Ask students to identify the themes for the passage.
- Have students read the themes in the box and choose the one that best describes the theme of the passage. (*trusting others* or *being in a group is better than being alone*)
- Have them draw and fill in a theme chart in their books.
- Invite students to draw a completed theme chart on the board and to explain their thinking to the class. Redirect as necessary.

Student page 112 ▶ **With a Partner**

Have students work together through a short passage.
- Draw attention to the boldfaced instructions and ask a volunteer to read them aloud.
- Point out to students that one question is below the passage and the other four are on the next page.
- Have students turn back to page 112. Have them read the passage in pairs and answer only the first question together. (1. D)
- Regroup as a class. Ask students to share their thoughts with the class.
- Ask students to explain the lesson they think the characters learned. (They are both brave in their own ways.) Redirect as necessary.

Tip

Tell students to focus on the main character or characters when deciding on the theme.

Student page 113 ▶ **On Your Own**

Have students work independently to answer more questions about the same passage.
- After students answer the questions, regroup as a class and ask them to explain their answer choices. (2. A 3. B 4. D 5. B) Redirect as necessary.

Think About

Have the students review the tools they've learned before beginning the On Your Own activity.

English Language Learners

Many of the theme words may be difficult to understand. Help English language learners comprehend the themes by inviting them to illustrate the list of themes on the board or chart paper, to be displayed while students are studying theme. For example, for *working hard leads to success,* students might illustrate a person practicing a certain sport.

Objective
To learn signal words that are sometimes used in questions about literary elements.

Coaching Tip

Explain to students that a simile always uses the signal words *like* or *as* to make comparisons.

▶ **Review the Skill**
Review how to find literary elements and the tools students have learned.

Ask	Write
Which comparison is a simile?	*Orange sun a ball*
Which comparison is a metaphor?	*Coach, like a dog, barks orders to avoid a loss.*

▶ **Learn the Vocabulary**
Students learn about signal words that identify questions about literary elements.

- Have a student read the question. Direct students' attention to *compared*. Tell them that *compared* is a signal word that shows the question is asking about a literary element.
- Then have students identify and underline the similes and identify and circle the metaphor.
- Invite them to explain how they knew what to underline and circle.

Signal Words	
simile	like
metaphor	as
represents	
compares	
comparison	

Check Back

Tell students to turn to page 32 to remember what a simile and metaphor chart looks like.

▶ **Apply the Vocabulary**
Have students identify the signal words in the question and use them to identify the simile.

- Ask students to place a box around the signal words in question 2. (*simile, comparison*)
- Have students draw and fill in a chart in their books.
- Invite students to draw a completed simile and metaphor chart on the board and explain their thinking to the class. Redirect as necessary.

Tip

Look for details in the descriptions of objects to understand the meaning of a simile or a metaphor.

▶ **With a Partner**
Have students work together and discuss their thinking while working through a short passage.

- Draw attention to the boldfaced instructions and ask a volunteer to read them aloud.
- Point out to students that one question is below the passage and the other four are on the next page. Have them draw a box around the signal word in the first question. (1. *compared*)
- Have pairs of students read the passage and answer only the first question together. (1. C)
- Regroup pairs of students as a class. Ask students to share which literary elements they found in the passage. (paragraph 1: simile: *rumbles like distant thunder* paragraph 2: metaphor: *ocean currents are gentle hands*; simile: *swims as quietly as a whisper* paragraph 3: metaphor: *muscles are knotted ropes*; simile: *waters are soothing like a warm bath*; metaphor: *they will become two gray ships*)
- Encourage them to explain the literary elements. Redirect as necessary.

Think About

Have students review the tools they've learned before beginning the On Your Own activity.

▶ **On Your Own**
Have students work independently to answer more questions about the same passage.

- After students answer the questions, regroup as a class and ask students which signal words they found in the questions. (2. *represents* 3. *compared* 4. *metaphor* 5. *as*)
- Then have them explain their answer choices. (2. B 3. D 4. C 5. B) Redirect as necessary.

English Language Learners

Ask each student to illustrate either a simile or a metaphor. Students can make a drawing or a sculpture using materials of their choice. Have students explain their work to classmates.

Objective

To use structural element signal words to identify structural element questions and to find the relationships in passages.

▶ **Review the Skill**

Review how to use a title, table of contents, heading, subheading, and index to help identify what a book, chapter, or passage will be about.

▶ **Learn the Vocabulary**

Signal Words	
index	subheading
title	heading
chapter	table of contents

Coaching Tip

Tell students that an index is a key part of a book that can help them find specific topics in the book.

Students learn about signal words that help them identify questions that ask about key parts of a book.

- Have students read the table of contents, passage, and question.
- Have students tell what they think the chapters will be about.
- Direct students' attention to the boxed signal word *chapter* in the question. Tell them *chapter* is a signal word that tells them the question is asking about that key part of the book.
- Call on a volunteer to answer the question. (B) Ask students to explain how they knew in which chapter the passage would be found. (the passage talks about fishing and boating)

▶ **Apply the Vocabulary**

Have students complete the activity.

- Have students read the table of contents and passage again.
- Ask a volunteer to draw a box around the heading in the passage. (*Striper Lake*)
- Ask students to identify the heading. (*Striper Lake*)

▶ **With a Partner**

Have students work together through a short passage.

- Draw attention to the boldfaced instructions and ask a volunteer to read them aloud.
- Point out to students that one question is below the passage and the other four are on the next page. Have them draw a box around the signal word in the first question. (1. *chapter*)
- Have pairs of students read the passage and answer only the first question. (1. C)
- Ask students to explain their answer choices. Redirect as necessary.

Tip

Point out to students that when they see a chapter title, they need to think about what the chapter might be about.

▶ **On Your Own**

Have students work independently to answer more questions about the same passage.

- After students answer the questions, regroup as a class, and ask students to identify signal words in the questions. (2. *chapter* 3. *chapter* 4. *chapter* 5. *heading*)
- Then have students regroup as a class and ask them to explain their answer choices. Redirect as necessary. (2. D 3. C 4. A 5. C)

Think About

Have students review the tools they've learned before beginning the On Your Own activity.

English Language Learners

Have students finish sentences to understand how to interpret titles and chapter headings. For example: The chapter titled *"Special Things About Shade Trees" might tell me about* . . . (leaves, animals that live in trees).

Objective

To learn the names of graphics and their key parts and to identify questions about visual information.

Student page 120 ▶ **Review the Skill**

Review with students that graphics can give you information that is not found in a passage. Look at the pictures, read the captions, study the charts, and read the time lines to see what they tell you.

▶ **Learn the Vocabulary**

Coaching Tip

Tell students that by first reading a graph's title and column headings and looking at the rows, they will have a good idea of what the graph is showing.

Students learn about the names of graphics and their key parts.

- Have a student read the question below the graph. Direct students' attention to *graph*. Tell them that *graph* is a name of a graphic.
- Then have students answer the question and explain their answer. (C)

▶ **Apply the Vocabulary**

Have students find and draw a box around key words.

- Ask students to draw a box around the words in the question and on the graph that help answer the question.

Key Words	
chart	column
graphic	caption
map	picture
row	graph
time line	key

Student page 121 ▶ **With a Partner**

Have students work together through a short passage.

Tip

Remind students that the captions underneath pictures, diagrams, and charts often contain important information.

- Draw attention to the boldfaced instructions and ask a volunteer to read them aloud.
- Point out to students that one question is below the passage and the other four are on the next page. Have them draw a box around the key word in the first question. (1. *caption*)
- Have pairs of students read the passage and answer only the first question. (1. C)
- Have volunteers share which signal word they found in the passage (paragraph 3: *picture*) and explain their thinking. Redirect as necessary.

Student page 122 ▶ **On Your Own**

Have students work independently to answer more questions about the same passage.

Think About

Have students review the tools they've learned before beginning the On Your Own activity.

- After students answer the questions, regroup as a class and ask students which words in the questions signaled visual information. (2. *picture* 3. *graphic* 5. *pictures*) Have them explain their answer choices. (2. A 3. C 4. A 5. B) Redirect as necessary.

English Language Learners

Have students finish the following sentence to get a feeling for how to interpret what tables, charts, and photos may mean. *In the picture of the goldfish, I can see . . .*

Objective
To use nonfiction writing signal words to identify types of nonfiction writing.

Student page 123

Coaching Tip

Tell students that informative writing rarely uses the words *I*, *we*, or *you*.

▶ **Review the Skill**
Review how to identify the types of nonfiction writing and the tools students have learned. Remind them that a biography is a true story about someone's life. Persuasive writing tries to convince the reader to think or act in a certain way. Functional writing gives step-by-step instructions. Informative writing gives information and facts.

▶ **Learn the Vocabulary**
Students learn about signal words that help them identify the purposes of nonfiction writing.
  ● Have a student read the first sentence in the passage. Direct students' attention to the word *think*. Tell them that *think* is a signal word that shows an opinion. Most persuasive writing includes the author's opinion.
  ● Then have students identify the other signal words in the passage. (*should, must, should*)
  ● Invite students to explain why these words signal persuasive writing.

Check Back

Tell students to turn to page 42 to remember what a nonfiction writing purpose chart looks like.

▶ **Apply the Vocabulary**
Have students find the signal words in the question that follows the passage and draw a box around them. (*think, should, feel*)
  ● Ask students to draw and complete a nonfiction writing purpose chart in their books.
  ● Invite a volunteer to draw his completed chart on the board and to explain his thinking. Redirect as necessary.

Signal Words
biography: born, died, lived, grew up, (people's names)
persuasive: feel/feeling/feels/felt; think/thinks/thought; do/does; should, must, have to
functional: first, then, finally, last, next, how, directions, instructions
informative: what, why, how

Student page 124

Tip

Point out to students that functional nonfiction writing often includes numbered steps.

▶ **With a Partner**
Have students work through a short passage together.
  ● Draw attention to the boldfaced instructions and ask a volunteer to read them aloud.
  ● Point out to students that one question is below the passage and the other four are on the next page.
  ● Have pairs of students read the passage and answer only the first question together. (1. B)
  ● Have volunteers share which signal words they found in the passage (paragraph 1: *directions, how to* paragraph 2: *directions, step* paragraph 3: *directions, then*) and explain their thinking. Redirect as necessary.

Student page 125

Think About

Have students review the tools they've learned before beginning the On Your Own activity.

▶ **On Your Own**
Have students work independently to answer more questions about the same passage.
  ● After students answer the questions, regroup as a class and ask students which words signaled types of nonfiction writing. (signal words 5. *how to*) Have students explain their answer choices. (2. B 3. A 4. D 5. C) Redirect as necessary.

English Language Learners
Have students finish the following sentence frames using a signal word. *Our class . . .* (feels that recess is not long enough). *Take out the peanut butter, . . .* (then spread it on the bread). *George Washington was . . .* (born in Virginia).

Answers

Hail

1. A Incorrect. This very general heading does not say anything about how hail is made.
   B Incorrect. This heading suggests a general description of hail.
   C **Correct. This heading suggests that the text will tell how hail is made.**
   D Incorrect. This heading suggests only the effects of hail, not how it is made.

2. A **Correct. The passage provides information about hail.**
   B Incorrect. The passage does not attempt to persuade the reader to dislike hail.
   C Incorrect. The passage does not instruct how to make hail.
   D Incorrect. Although the passage talks about the damage caused by hail, that is not the purpose of the passage.

3. A Incorrect. The passage and diagram do not indicate that the layers tell anything about the air temperature.
   B Incorrect. Nothing in the passage or diagram indicates that the layers tell about the size of the cloud the hailstone came from.
   C Incorrect. Nothing in the passage or diagram indicates that the layers tell about the kind of cloud the hailstone came from.
   D **Correct. The caption for the diagram tells about the movement of the hailstone inside the cloud.**

A First Job

4. A **Correct. Paragraph 2 states *Marcus seemed to have faith that he would do fine.***
   B Incorrect. Lee gets along with his boss.
   C Incorrect. The passage does not include any information to support this.
   D Incorrect. Paragraph 2 suggests that Lee finds the job challenging.

5. A **Correct. The first sentence says he got a job, and the last sentence shows he was successfully flipping pancakes.**
   B Incorrect. This is only one event, not the plot.
   C Incorrect. This is only the beginning.
   D Incorrect. This is only one event.

6. A Incorrect. Lee is not a machine. This is not a reason for the comparison.
   B Incorrect. Lee does not make cars. This is not a reason for the comparison.
   C Incorrect. Lee may like pancakes, but an assembly line does not. This is not a reason for the comparison.
   D **Correct. Lee is compared to an assembly line because he, like an assembly line, moves quickly.**

7. A Incorrect. The passage never indicates this.
   B **Correct. Paragraph 1 states that *Lee was excited* and his *heart leapt a bit.***
   C Incorrect. Lee is never impolite.
   D Incorrect. Paragraph 2 states that he was enjoying the challenge.

Unit 3: Vocabulary

Student page 128 ▶

Student page 128

Root words, prefixes, and suffixes
Synonyms and antonyms
Context clues
Multiple-meaning words

Introducing the Unit

Have students look at the list of vocabulary skills. Have students read each skill aloud. To activate prior knowledge, ask students if they remember the meaning of each skill.

- Ask *What are root words, prefixes, and suffixes? How can these help you understand unfamiliar words?* Discuss student responses.
- Ask *What is a synonym? What is an antonym? How are these helpful to you when you read?* Discuss student responses.
- Ask *What are context clues? Can someone explain how a reader would use this skill?* Discuss student responses.
- Ask *What is a multiple-meaning word? How do you know which meaning of a word to use?* Discuss student responses.

Have students practice using vocabulary skills by asking them the following questions.

- Ask *What does the prefix* dis- *mean? Give an example of a root word that has had the prefix* dis- *added to it.* Discuss student responses.
- Ask *What does the suffix* -less *mean? Give an example of a root word that has had the suffix* -less *added to it.* Discuss student responses.
- Say *Listen to this word:* revisit. *What is the root word? What is the prefix?* Discuss student responses.
- Ask *What is a synonym for the word* scary? *What is a synonym for the word* pretty? Discuss student responses.
- Ask *What is an antonym for the word* long? *What is an antonym for the word* easy? Discuss student responses.
- Say *Listen to this sentence: It was a lonesome night for Richard, who was all by himself. What does the word* lonesome *mean? What context clues helped you figure out the meaning of the word?* Discuss student responses.
- Ask *What are two meanings of the word* slide? Discuss student responses.
- Ask *What are some multiple-meaning words you can think of?* Discuss student responses.

Remind students that they will continue to learn how to use these skills. Then explain that at the end of the unit they will have an opportunity to do a personal evaluation of what they learned.

Examples:

Root words, prefixes, and suffixes: The suffix *-ful* means "full of," so *thankful* means "full of thanks."

Synonyms and antonyms: A synonym for *easy* is *simple*. An antonym for *easy* is *difficult*.

Context clues: *Because of Jim's gregarious personality, he knew many people.* You can understand that the word *gregarious* means "outgoing" or "friendly" from the rest of the sentence.

Multiple-meaning words: The word *steer* means "to control something" and "male cow."

At the End of the Unit

When students finish the skills in this unit, have them return to this page and complete the exercise at the bottom. In this activity, your students will reflect on the following three things:

- what they learned
- what they feel good about
- what they feel they need more practice with

This exercise makes learning personal and allows students to reflect on what they've learned. Ask students to be active learners. Help them understand that they are responsible for their own learning.

Objective

To identify root words, prefixes, and suffixes and associate them with their meanings.

Student page 129 ▶ **Review the Skill**

Coaching Tip

Tell students that they should look for root words, prefixes, and suffixes in new words that they find in their reading.

Review how to identify root words, prefixes, and suffixes and the tools students have learned. Give examples and ask students to identify the root word, prefix, or suffix. Example: *What is the root word in* unreadable? (read) *What is the prefix in* unreadable? (un-) *What is the suffix in* unreadable? (-able) *What is the meaning of* unreadable? (not able to read)

Learn the Vocabulary

Students identify root words, prefixes, and suffixes and use them to decide the meanings of words.

- Have a student read the first sentence in the passage. Direct students' attention to *careful*. Tell them to separate this word into a root word and suffix to discover its meaning.
- Have students identify and underline the root word and identify and circle the suffix. (root word: *care*, suffix: *-ful*) Ask them to combine the meaning of the word parts and give the meaning of *careful*. (full of care)
- Continue in the same way to have students identify the word parts and meanings of *unsure* and *replace*.

Check Back

Tell students to turn to page 48 for a chart of prefixes, suffixes, and their meanings.

Apply the Vocabulary

Have students draw and fill in a prefix, root word, suffix, and meaning chart. (*care*, *-ful*, *full of care*; *un-*, *sure*, *not sure*; *re-*, *place*, *place again*)

- Invite students to share their completed root word, prefix, suffix, and meaning charts on the board and explain their thinking to the class. Redirect as necessary.
- Have students write a sentence in their books using each shaded word. Ask volunteers to share their sentences.

Student page 130 ▶ **With a Partner**

Tip

Remind students to use the meanings of root words, prefixes, and suffixes to figure out the meanings of new words.

Have students work together and discuss their thinking while working through a short passage.

- Draw attention to the boldface instructions and ask a volunteer to read them aloud.
- Point out to students that one question is below the passage and the other four are on the next page.
- Have pairs of students read the passage and answer only the first question together. (1. C)
- Regroup as a class. Ask students to explain their answer choice. Have volunteers share what word parts they wrote in their charts and explain their thinking. Redirect as necessary.

Student page 131 ▶ **On Your Own**

Think About

Have students review the tools they've learned before beginning the On Your Own activity.

Have students work independently to answer more questions about the same passage.

- After students answer the questions, regroup as a class and ask students to explain their answer choices. (2. C 3. A 4. D 5. D) Redirect as necessary. Ask students how they figured out the answers.

English Language Learners

Have students refer to the chart they made for the passage on page 130. Stress to them that adding prefixes and suffixes to root words changes the meaning of those words. Ask students to explain what each of the root words in the chart means. Then ask them to explain how the definitions change with the addition of prefixes or suffixes.

Objective

To identify synonyms and antonyms and to learn words that signal questions about synonyms and antonyms.

Student page 132 ▶ **Review the Skill**

Review how to identify synonyms and antonyms and the tools students learned on page 50.

- Write the following synonyms on the board: *small, tiny, little.* Ask *Do these words mean the same or opposite?* (They are synonyms. They have similar meanings.)
- Say *Name some words that mean the opposite of these words* (*antonyms*). Write examples on the board: *large, big, great, huge.*
- Remind students that synonyms and antonyms can be clues to the meanings of other words.

Coaching Tip

Point out to students that writers sometimes include a nearby synonym or antonym when they introduce a word that may be unknown to readers.

▶ **Learn the Vocabulary**

Students learn about signal words that identify synonyms and antonyms.

- Have a student read the passage. Direct students' attention to *species.* Ask students to think about the word's meaning.
- Have students read question 1 that follows the passage. Direct students' attention to the words *same as* in the question. Tell them that these words are signal words that identify synonyms.
- Have students look for another word in the passage with the same meaning as *species.* Invite them to explain their answers.

Signal Words	
synonym	same as
antonym	different
similar	alike
opposite	unlike

Check Back

Tell students to turn to page 50 for an example of a synonym and antonym chart.

▶ **Apply the Vocabulary**

- Have students read the passage again and draw a box around the signal word in question 2. (*opposite*)
- Ask students to identify the antonym of the underlined word and answer the question. (2. B)

Student page 133 ▶ **With a Partner**

Have students discuss their thinking while working through a short passage together.

- Draw attention to the boldface instructions and ask a volunteer to read them aloud.
- Point out to students that one question is below the passage and the other four are on the next page. Have them draw a box around the signal words in the first question. (*the same as*)
- Have pairs of students read the passage and answer only the first question together. (1. B)

Tip

Tell students to look for nearby synonyms and antonyms to help them understand new words.

Student page 134 ▶ **On Your Own**

Ask students to work independently to answer more questions about the same passage.

- After students answer the questions, regroup as a class and ask students what synonyms and antonyms helped them with word meanings.
- Have students explain their answer choices. (2. A 3. D 4. C 5. A) Redirect as necessary.

Think About

Have students review the tools they've learned before beginning the On Your Own activity.

English Language Learners

Write the signal words on index cards and give them to students. Have them group the words into synonyms and antonyms. Then hold up pairs of simple words and have students choose a signal word from their groups to make a sentence. For example, with the word pair *big* and *small*, a student could write *Big is unlike small.* Choose enough word pairs to use all of the signal words.

Objective

To find context clues in a passage and to identify the types of context clues in order to define an unfamiliar word.

Student page 135
▶ **Review the Skill**

Review how to find context clues and how to use the tools students have learned.

Say *The context of a new word is the words and sentences around it. A context clue is text that gives you a hint to the meaning of the new word. For example, if I read the sentence* Bacteria and other germs can make people sick, *I can figure out that* bacteria *are a type of* germ *and that one definition of* bacteria *is "a germ that can make you sick."*

Coaching Tip

Tell students that if a context clue is a synonym, they can replace the unfamiliar word with the synonym and the sentence will have the same meaning.

▶ **Learn the Vocabulary**

Students learn about the types of context clues that help them decipher the meaning of an unfamiliar word.

- Have a student read the first sentence of the passage. Direct students' attention to the underlined word *revolves*.
- Have students identify the circled context clue for *revolves* and determine what type of clue it is. (context clue: *go around*; type of context clue: restatement)
- Invite students to explain their thinking. Then have students read the rest of the passage.

Signal Words	
comparison	example
restatement	synonym

Check Back

Tell students to turn to page 53 to remember what a clues chart looks like.

▶ **Apply the Vocabulary**

Have students look for another context clue and draw a circle around it.

- Ask students to identify and draw a circle around the context clue for *crescent* in the fifth sentence of the passage. (*or curved shape*) Ask students to identify the type of context clue (restatement) and answer the questions. Then have them draw and fill in a clues chart.
- Invite students to share their answers. (a *crescent* is a *curved shape*; some clues might be *look like, curved shape,* and *entire moon*)

Student page 136
▶ **With a Partner**

Have students discuss their thinking while working through a short passage.

Tip

A context clue that compares may use the words *like* or *same as* after the unfamiliar word.

- Draw attention to the boldface instructions and ask a volunteer to read them aloud.
- Point out to students that one question is below the passage and the other four are on the next page.
- Have pairs of students read the passage and answer only the first question. (1. A)
- Have volunteers share what context clues they found in the passage. (paragraph 1: resemble—*alike*; paragraph 2: particular—*live in only one kind of tree*; paragraph 3: dens—*or their homes*, reside—*also live in*; paragraph 4: varieties—*ants, termites, beetles, butterflies, and other bugs*)
- Encourage them to explain how they found the context clues. Redirect as necessary.

Student page 137
▶ **On Your Own**

Have students work independently to answer more questions about the same passage.

Think About

Have students review the tools they have learned before beginning the On Your Own activity.

- After students answer the questions, regroup as a class and ask students how they determined what type each context clue is. Then have students explain their answer choices. (2. A 3. C 4. B 5. D) Redirect as necessary.

English Language Learners

Have students play a game of charades and give clues to guess different words. Example: *chicken: clucking, egg, flapping wings* or *car: driving, engine roar.*

Objective
To identify the multiple-meaning words in a passage and determine their correct meaning.

Student page 138 ▶ **Review the Skill**
Review how to identify multiple-meaning words and how to use the tools students have learned. Remind them that multiple-meaning words have more than one meaning. Give examples and ask students to identify the correct meaning. For example, *The music teacher wrote a note to ask the students to play the last note longer.*

Coaching Tip

Tell students that when a sentence seems confusing they can try substituting a different meaning for the word to see if it makes sense.

▶ **Learn the Vocabulary**
Students learn about signal words that identify questions about multiple-meaning words.

- Have a student read the passage. Direct students' attention to *rich*. Students should determine that *rich* is used here to mean "full of good things."
- Have students read the question. Direct students to the signal words *which meaning*. Tell them that these words signal that the question is asking about a multiple-meaning word.

Signal Words
which definition
look at the definition
which meaning
makes the most sense

Check Back

Tell students to turn to page 56 to remember what a multiple-meaning word chart looks like.

▶ **Apply the Vocabulary**
Have students read the passage again.

- Direct students' attention to the word *level*.
- Ask students to think about the different meanings of the word and what meanings make the most sense.
- Ask students to draw a box around the signal words in the question.
- Invite students to answer the question (2. A) and share their answer choices. Redirect as necessary.
- Ask volunteers to complete a multiple-meaning word chart on the board and explain their thinking to the class. Redirect as necessary.

Student page 139 ▶ **With a Partner**
Have students work together and discuss their thinking while working through a short passage.

- Draw attention to the boldface instructions and ask a volunteer to read them aloud.
- Point out to students that one question is below the passage and the other three are on the next page.
- Have pairs of students read the passage and answer only the first question. (1. C)
- Have volunteers share how they decided which word belonged in the blank for both sentences. Redirect as necessary.

Tip

Point out to students that they can use clues in a sentence to help them figure out the meaning of a word.

Student page 140 ▶ **On Your Own**
Have students work independently to answer more questions about the same passage.

- After students answer the questions, regroup as a class and ask students how they determined the correct meaning for each multiple-meaning word. Have them explain their answer choices. (2. B 3. D 4. C) Redirect as necessary.

Think About

Have students review the tools they've learned before beginning the On Your Own activity.

English Language Learners

Have students use multiple-meaning words to construct a silly story as a group. Write a list of simple words on the board to start them off, such as *rock, mine, flap, story, close, tip,* or *pound.* To help them use the words correctly, have them give different meanings for the words. Then have them write sentences. An example of a silly story might be: *I tossed a rock into a mine. The mine started to rock. My hat fell into the mine. I had to get it because it was mine.*

Answers

Setting Up a Bird Feeder

1. A Incorrect. *Observe* does not mean to buy birds.
   B **Correct. *Watch* is a synonym for *observe*.**
   C Incorrect. *Move* is not a synonym for *observe*.
   D Incorrect. *Improve* is not a synonym for *observe.*

2. A Incorrect. *Small* is not the meaning of *sizeable.*
   B Incorrect. *Sick* does not refer to size.
   C **Correct. *Sizeable* means the size is impressive, or large.**
   D Incorrect. *Sighing* does not refer to size.

3. A Incorrect. *Prefer* and *think about* do not mean the same thing, so they are not synonyms.
   B **Correct. *Like best* has a similar meaning to *prefer.***
   C Incorrect. *Prefer* and *eat a lot of* do not mean the same thing, so they are not synonyms.
   D Incorrect. *Prefer* and *pick at* do not mean the same thing, so they are not synonyms.

4. A Incorrect. *Superior* has a similar meaning to *superb*, not the opposite.
   B **Correct. *Awful* means the opposite of *superb*.**
   C Incorrect. *Superb* does not refer to health.
   D Incorrect. *Superb* does not refer to expense.

5. A Incorrect. *Position* does not mean *job* in this sentence.
   B Incorrect. *Position* does not mean *rank* in this sentence.
   C **Correct. *Location* and *position* mean the same thing.**
   D Incorrect. *Position* does not mean *opinion* in this sentence.

Unit 4: Critical Thinking

Student page 142 ▶ **Introducing the Unit**

Student page 142

Author's purpose
Facts and opinions
Draw conclusions
    and make
    inferences
Make predictions
Summarize

Have students look at the list of critical-thinking skills found on page 142 of Unit 4. Have students read each skill aloud. To activiate prior knowledge, ask students if they remember the meaning of each skill.

Read aloud the following sentences and then have students identify the critical-thinking skill being used.

- Say *You should go to Hawaii. Hawaii has warm weather, nice beaches, and friendly people. You will have a great time in Hawaii.* Ask students *What is the author's purpose in writing this passage?* Have volunteers share their responses with the class.
- Say *The King Cobra is a poisonous snake. It lives in Asia. It is the most beautiful snake of them all.* Ask students *Which information is a fact? Which information is an opinion?* Have volunteers share their responses with the class.
- Say *Aruna got up early and cleaned her room. Then she tidied up the kitchen. She also cleaned the front room.* Ask students *What conclusion can you make about Aruna?* Have volunteers share their responses with the class.
- Say *Barry practiced the trumpet every day after school. He wanted to be in the school band. He knew how to play every note. On Tuesday, he would play his trumpet for the music teacher, Mr. Dawkins.* Ask students *What do you predict will happen next?* Have volunteers share their responses with the class.
- Say *The modern hamburger has no clear inventor. One person claimed to invent the hamburger bun in 1921. Cheeseburgers were invented in 1924. Hamburgers are found in many countries around the world.* Say *How would we summarize this passage?* Discuss answers with students.

Remind students that they will continue to learn how to use these skills. Then explain that at the end of the unit they will have an opportunity to do a personal evaluation of what they have learned.

Examples:

Author's purpose: An author wrote a funny book in order to entertain the reader.

Facts and opinions: The U.S. government recommends walking for 30 minutes every day. I think we should have recess every day for an hour.

Draw conclusions and make inferences: Kevin wants to enter the city bike race. To prepare, he rides his bike every day for one hour. Even if the weather is bad, he rides his bike. I can conclude that Kevin is a very determined person.

Make predictions: Molly and Beth have known each other since first grade. They eat lunch together every day. They even do fun things on the weekend. I predict that Molly and Beth will stay friends for a long time.

Summarize: Stars are large balls of glowing, hot gas. Most stars are made of hydrogen and helium. Stars come in different sizes, colors, and temperatures.

At the End of the Unit

When students finish the skills in this unit, have them return to this page and complete the exercise at the bottom. In this activity, your students will reflect on the following three things:

- what they learned
- what they feel good about
- what they feel they need more practice with

This exercise makes learning personal and allows students to reflect on what they've learned. Ask students to be active learners. Help them understand that they are responsible for their own learning.

Objective
To use author's purpose signal words to identify the author's purpose.

Student page 143

Coaching Tip

Tell students that if they see *I think* or *I believe*, the author is expressing an opinion.

Check Back

Tell students to look at the chart on page 61 to see the different purposes an author may have.

▶ **Review the Skill**

Review how to find the author's purpose and the tools students have learned. Remind them that the author's purpose is the reason the author wrote the passage. Give examples and ask students to identify the author's purpose. For example: Tell students about something funny that you recently read. Ask students to determine the author's primary reason for writing the passage.

▶ **Learn the Vocabulary**

Students learn about signal words that help them identify the author's purpose.

- Have a student read the first paragraph of the passage. Direct students' attention to *Jumbo the Jet and Retro the Rocket* and *sat on a shelf*. Tell them that these words are signal words that show the author's purpose.

Signal Words	
To persuade	opinion words
	value comparisons
To inform	facts, figures, directions
To entertain	characters and events
To express feelings	feeling words

▶ **Apply the Vocabulary**

- Have students find the signal words in the last paragraph of the passage. (*Retro, Tony, picked us*)
- Have them look at the chart above the passage. Point out to students that *Jumbo the Jet* and *Retro the Rocket* are characters and *sat on a shelf* is an event. According to the chart, the author's purpose for this passage is to entertain.

Student page 144

Tip

Tell students that signal words are clues to the author's purpose.

▶ **With a Partner**

Have students work together and discuss their thinking while working through a short passage.

- Draw attention to the boldface instructions and ask a volunteer to read them aloud.
- Point out to students that one question is below the passage and the other four are on the next page.
- Have pairs of students read the passage and answer only the first question. (1. A)
- Invite volunteers to share which signal words they found in the passage (answers will vary) and to explain their thinking. Redirect as necessary.

Student page 145

Think About

Have students review the tools they've learned before beginning the On Your Own activity.

▶ **On Your Own**

Have students work independently to answer more questions about the same passage.

- Have students explain their answer choices. (2. C 3. B 4. D 5. B) Redirect as necessary.

English Language Learners

Put students into small groups with a poster board divided into four sections for each author's purpose. (to persuade, inform, entertain, express feelings) Give students sentences on pieces of paper and have them put each sentence into the correct author's purpose section. Have students highlight the signal words in each sentence and explain their thinking.

Objective
To use fact and opinion signal words to identify opinions in passages.

Student page 146 ▶ **Review the Skill**

Review how to find facts and opinions and the tools students have learned.

Say *A fact can be proved true. An opinion tells how someone feels or believes.* Say *The sun rose at 5:32 this morning. Sunrise is the most beautiful part of the day.* Invite students to identify the fact and the opinion. Then ask students to give a similar example of a fact and an opinion.

Coaching Tip

Tell students that writers often use opinion signal words to persuade the readers to see their thinking about a subject.

▶ **Learn the Vocabulary**

Students learn about signal words that help them identify opinions.

- Have a student read the first sentence in the passage. Direct students' attention to *amazing*. Tell them that *amazing* is a signal word that shows the sentence is an opinion.
- Have students identify and circle another opinion and underline a fact. (Fact: *Flowers begin to bloom, birds begin to sing, and the sun shines brightly.* Opinion: *When spring arrives, you can do fun things outside.*)
- Invite them to explain how they knew what to underline and circle.

> **Signal Words**
>
> **Words that make a comparison:** best, greatest, worse, better
> **Words that show a belief:** believe, feel, think
> **Words that describe quality:** amazing, beautiful, interesting, difficult

Check Back

Tell students to turn to page 65 to remember what a fact and opinion chart looks like.

▶ **Apply the Vocabulary**

Have students find and draw a box around the signal words.

- Ask students to identify and draw a box around the signal words in the last sentence of the same passage. (*I believe, best*) Ask students to identify the fact and opinion sentences in the second paragraph and have them draw and fill in a fact and opinion chart.
- Invite students to share their answers and to explain their thinking to the class. Redirect as necessary.

Student page 147 ▶ **With a Partner**

Have students work and discuss their thinking while working through a short passage.

- Draw attention to the boldface instructions and ask a volunteer to read them aloud.
- Point out to students that one question is below the passage and the other four are on the next page.
- Have pairs of students read the passage and answer only the first question. (1. D)
- Have volunteers share which signal words they found in the passage (paragraph 1: *interesting*; paragraph 2: *most, greatest*; paragraph 3: *best, most* paragraph 5: *amazing, beautiful, exciting*) Redirect as necessary.

Tip

Tell students that when a question asks for something that can be proved true, it is asking for a fact.

Student page 148 ▶ **On Your Own**

Have students work independently to answer more questions about the same passage.

- Have them explain their answer choices. (2. B 3. C 4. D 5. A) Redirect as necessary.

Think About

Have students review the tools they've learned before beginning the On Your Own activity.

> ### English Language Learners
>
> Make two columns on the board. In one column, write *comparison, belief,* and *quality*. In the other column, write opinion words such as *best, gross, think,* and others. Have students come to the board and draw a line from an opinion word to its type. For example, a student would draw a line from *best* to *comparison*. Have students use the word they chose in a sentence.

Objective
To identify signal words and find details that help draw conclusions and make inferences.

Student page 149 ▶ **Review the Skill**
Review how to draw conclusions and make inferences and the tools students have learned. Say *You can use passage details to draw a conclusion. You can use details and what you know from real life to make an inference.* Provide examples, such as *I noticed a man with a brush and a bucket of paint by my neighbor's house. I can conclude he is painting the house. I heard a clock chime seven times. I know each chime means one hour. I can infer that it was 7:00.*

Coaching Tip

Tell students to organize their clues based on what the question asks about. For the question about Ruby, students should pay attention to sentences that mention Ruby.

▶ **Learn the Vocabulary**
Students learn about signal words in questions that tell them to draw a conclusion or make an inference.

Signal Words	
conclude	conclusion
infer	probably

- Have students read the passage and the question that follows. Point out that the word in the box is a signal word. Tell them they will be making an inference about Ruby.
- Have students identify details in the passage about Ruby. (*quickly placed, eager, stuck to her fingers, laughed at herself*)
- Ask students to share their answers for the details they located in the passage to support the inference that Ruby was sloppy and excited. Redirect as necessary.

Check Back

Tell students to turn to page 67 to remember what a conclusions and inferences chart looks like.

▶ **Apply the Vocabulary**
Students find the signal word and draw a box around it.

- Ask students what the signal word is in question 20 (*conclude*) and have them draw a box around it.
- Ask students to underline passage details that help them draw a conclusion about what Ruby is making. (*newspaper strips, cone-shaped model, wet paste, smoothed the paste, orange paper strips*)
- Have them answer the question (2. C) and share their thinking with the class. Redirect as necessary.

Student page 150 ▶ **With a Partner**
Have students work together through a short passage.

Tip

Remind students to combine what they already know with clues from the passage to make an inference.

- Draw attention to the boldfaced instructions and ask a volunteer to read them aloud.
- Point out to students that one question is below the passage and the other four are on the next page.
- Have pairs of students read the passage and answer only the first question. (1. B)
- Regroup as a class. Have volunteers share the story details that helped them draw a conclusion about how Adam felt about being in the library. (paragraph 1 *Deron left his friend, boys agreed to meet*) Redirect as necessary.

Student page 151 ▶ **On Your Own**
Have students work independently to answer more questions about the same passage.

Think About

Have students review the tools they've learned before beginning the On Your Own activity.

- After students answer the questions, regroup as a class and ask students which signal words they found. (*conclude, infer, conclude*)
- Have them explain their answer choices. (2. A 3. B 4. D 5. B) Redirect as necessary.

English Language Learners

Encourage students to ask classmates questions about unfamiliar vocabulary/concepts in the passage. For example, *drawings of armor, wheeled to a table, Middle Ages, pulled from the shelf, and so on.*)

Objective
To learn signal words that relate to making predictions and answer questions about making predictions.

Student page 152

Coaching Tip

Tell students that predicting is not the same thing as guessing. They have to use the evidence in a passage to make sure their prediction makes sense.

▶ Review the Skill
Review how to make predictions and identify tools that students have learned.
Say *When you make a prediction, you tell what you think is going to happen based on the information you have.* Say *I was going to meet a friend for dinner, but I couldn't find my car keys. She was waiting for me. I had to look for the keys for a long time.* Ask *Was I on time to meet my friend?* (No) *How did my friend probably feel?* (I was late. My friend was upset.)

Learn the Vocabulary
Students will learn words that signal making predictions.

- Have students read the passage.
- Direct students to the signal words boxed in the question. Tell them that the words signal that they should make a prediction.
- Direct them to underline the clues that help them predict what Denis will probably do next. (*He promised his grandmother, she could depend on Denis, he knew he should keep his promise.*)

Signal Words	
clues	evidence
happen next	likely
predict	probably do

Check Back

Tell students to turn to page 70 to recall what a predictions web looks like.

Apply the Vocabulary
Have students find the signal words in the question and then answer the question.

- Have students read the question and draw a box around the signal word.
- Direct students to draw a predictions web and fill it in.
- Direct students to answer the question using the web (2. D). Ask students to share their responses and explain their thinking. Redirect as necessary.

Student page 153

Tip

Tell students to use the clues in the passage to predict what will happen next.

▶ With a Partner
Have students work together through a short passage.

- Draw attention to the boldface instructions and ask a volunteer to read them aloud.
- Point out that one question is below the passage and four are on the next page.
- Have them draw a box around the signal word in the question. (1. *predicts*)
- Have students read the passage in pairs and answer only the first question. (1. B)
- Have volunteers share which clues they found in the passage.
- Encourage them to explain related clues/predictions relationships. Redirect as necessary.

Student page 154

Think About

Have students review the tools they've learned before beginning the On Your Own activity.

▶ On Your Own
Have students work independently to answer more questions about the same passage.

- After students answer the questions, regroup as a class and ask students which signal words they found in the rest of the questions. (2. *likely* 3. *clues, prediction* 4. *likely* 5. *clue*)
- Then have them explain their answer choices. (2. B 3. A 4. A 5. C) Redirect as necessary.

English Language Learners

Have students finish scenarios by making a prediction. Example: *My family went camping and brought cans of food. We forgot to bring a can opener. The group next to us had a can opener. What happens next?*

Objective

To identify the information that should be included in a summary and answer questions about summarizing.

Student page 155

▶ **Review the Skill**

A summary explains the most important parts of a passage in fewer words, including all of the main ideas.

- Ask a volunteer to describe an activity he or she really enjoys. Then ask him or her to give several reasons why he or she enjoys that activity.
- Write *[student name] really likes [activity]. He or she thinks it is [list reasons].*
- Have other students help you circle the main idea, underline other important information, and complete a summary web. Ask a volunteer to summarize the information.

Coaching Tip

Tell students to find main ideas first and then look for other details to include in a summary.

▶ **Learn the Vocabulary**

Students learn a strategy that will help them identify the information that should be included in a summary.

- Review what should be included in a summary with the class. (all of the main ideas and other important information)
- Have students read the passage and circle the main idea in each paragraph and underline words that give other important information, such as answers to who, what, where, when, why, and how.
- Direct students to read each of the sample summaries but not the explanations.
- Have them compare what they have circled and underlined to what is included in the samples.
- Ask students which summary is best and why. Then have them discuss the explanations.

Check Back

Tell students to turn to page 73 to recall what a summary web looks like.

▶ **Apply the Vocabulary**

Have students reread the entire passage.

- Have students write their own summary of the passage on a separate sheet of paper, using the opening sentence supplied in their book. They should draw and fill in summary webs to help them write their summaries. (Answers will vary; the second summary under Learn the Vocabulary is a useful guide. Students should be encouraged to use their own words in a summary.)
- Invite students to compare their summaries and discuss whether they have included the most important information from the passage.
- Point out to students that summaries are rarely identical and can be worded in different ways, as long as the most important information is included.

Student page 156

▶ **With a Partner**

Have students work together through a short passage.

- Draw attention to the boldface instructions and ask a volunteer to read them aloud.
- Point out to students that one question is below the passage and the other three are on the next page.
- Have pairs of students read the passage and answer only the first question. (1. C)

Tip

Point out to students that a summary often has information from each paragraph.

Student page 157

▶ **On Your Own**

Have students work independently to answer more questions about the same passage.

- After students answer the questions, regroup as a class. Have them explain their answer choices. (2. A 3. A 4. B)

Think About

Have students review the tools they've learned before beginning the On Your Own activity.

English Language Learners

Ask students to talk about something they had to plan for, such as a vacation, a party, or a test. Have them explain how it was planned, what they had to do, and what happened.

Answers

Blia Trains Her Parakeet

1. A Incorrect. The passage does not discuss the amount of work required to train a bird.
   B Incorrect. While the passage may make the reader happy, this is not the focus of the passage.
   C Incorrect. The passage may even persuade the reader to *avoid* buying a bird.
   D **Correct. The passage gives clear tips on how to train a bird.**

2. A **Correct. This answer includes the most important parts of the passage and the main ideas.**
   B Incorrect. This answer includes details but not the most important parts of the passage.
   C Incorrect. This answer includes details but not the most important parts of the passage.
   D Incorrect. This answer includes details but not the most important parts of the passage.

3. A Incorrect. The information in the passage leads to the conclusion that Blia followed instructions on how to put her hand in the cage.
   B **Correct. The information in the passage leads to the conclusion that the parakeet did not feel safe around Blia.**
   C Incorrect. The passage indicates that Blia spoke softly to the parakeet.
   D Incorrect. The passage indicates that the parakeet eventually responded to Blia.

4. A Incorrect. This is a statement that cannot be proved true or false.
   B **Correct. This is true based on the events in the passage.**
   C Incorrect. This is an opinion that cannot be proved.
   D Incorrect. This is an opinion and it cannot be proved true or false.

5. A Incorrect. Pixie has already shown that she is no longer afraid of Blia.
   B Incorrect. This will not happen because Blia is already making progress on her own.
   C **Correct. The passage shows that Blia has gained confidence and understanding.**
   D Incorrect. There are no clues in the passage that suggest this will happen.

6. A Incorrect. The passage does not suggest that Blia's mother fears birds.
   B **Correct. Blia's mother is the person who helped her train the bird.**
   C Incorrect. Blia's mother gave her a book and advice, showing that she doesn't mind having the bird around.
   D Incorrect. Blia's mother's demeanor has been kind and patient, not annoyed.

Step 2 | Review

Answers

Rescue on the Beach

1. A **Correct. The children were very kind to an injured animal, and that made them happy.**
   B Incorrect. Evil is never mentioned in the passage.
   C Incorrect. Friendship is not discussed.
   D Incorrect. Being a winner is not the focus of the story.

2. A Incorrect. Jamal did not want to go to the game once they had seen the bird.
   B Incorrect. Ebony did not want to help the bird at first.
   C **Correct. Jamal wanted to help the bird and had to persuade Ebony to help.**
   D Incorrect. Ebony did not want to stay at the beach and miss the game.

3. A **Correct. The statement shows that the setting is the beach.**
   B Incorrect. It does not tell where or when the story took place.
   C Incorrect. It does not tell where or when the story took place.
   D Incorrect. It does not tell where or when the story took place.

4. A Incorrect. It shows only one part of the kind of person Jamal is.
   B Incorrect. It shows only one part of the kind of person Jamal is.
   C Incorrect. It does not show what kind of person Jamal is.
   D **Correct. It shows that Jamal is a caring person who does the right thing, even when it means giving up something he wants.**

5. A Incorrect. *Control* does not mean "power" here.
   B **Correct. *Control* describes a group that aids animals.**
   C Incorrect. *Control* does not have anything to do with an experiment here.
   D Incorrect. *Control* does not involve order here.

6. A Incorrect. This is true, but it is not the main idea.
   B Incorrect. This might be true, but the passage does not discuss which is more fun.
   C Incorrect. The passage does not discuss whether it is common to see injured animals on the beach.
   D **Correct. The children learned that it is best to call for help when they find an injured animal.**

7. A Incorrect. These are details but miss important actions.
   B **Correct. This summarizes the important things that happen in the first four paragraphs.**
   C Incorrect. They do not have to stop by the sand bank; they choose to.
   D Incorrect. This summary omits some important actions.

Life in a Castle

8. A Incorrect. The passage does not describe the author's views on specific castles.
   B Incorrect. The passage does not tell how to live in a castle.
   C **Correct. The passage gives information and facts on castle life.**
   D Incorrect. The passage does not tell a story about a lord and lady.

9. A **Correct. The keep, stables, and workshop are all within the curtain wall.**
   B Incorrect. These parts of the castle are not within the curtain wall.
   C Incorrect. The iron gate is not within the curtain wall.
   D Incorrect. The drawbridge and gatehouse are not within the curtain wall.

10. A Incorrect. Horses would not be kept in the sleeping chambers.
    B Incorrect. This section would describe rooms in the great tower.
    C Incorrect. This section would be about meals in the castle.
    D **Correct. "Parts of the Castle" would include the stables.**

11. A Incorrect. It cannot be proved. It is someone's belief.
    B **Correct. It is stated as a fact and can be proved by checking reference books.**
    C Incorrect. It cannot be proved. It is someone's belief.
    D Incorrect. It cannot be proved. It is someone's belief.

12. A Incorrect. This is not suggested or stated in the passage.
    B Incorrect. This is not suggested or stated in the passage.
    C Incorrect. This is not suggested or stated in the passage.
    D **Correct. All descriptions of the moat and drawbridge are tied to protecting the people inside from enemies.**

13. A. Incorrect. The passage does not indicate when they built a fire.

    B **Correct. The passage says, "Then they would get fruits and vegetables from the garden."**

    C Incorrect. They got the meat after they got the vegetables.

    D Incorrect. They cooked food after they got meat and vegetables.

14. A Incorrect. The passage does not say this.

    B Incorrect. This answer does not tell why the gatehouse was built for the door.

    C **Correct. The passage states that this is why the door was built into a gatehouse.**

    D Incorrect. This answer does not tell why the gatehouse was built for the door.

15. A Incorrect. *Chefs* refers to those who made the suppers, not the suppers themselves.

    B **Correct. *Cooks* means the same as *chefs*.**

    C Incorrect. *Meats* are what the chefs cooked.

    D Incorrect. *Tables* does not refer to people who cooked food.

Carlsbad Caverns National Park

16. A Incorrect. The passage gives clues that the photographs turned out.

    B Incorrect. The passage gives clues that the photographs were accepted.

    C Incorrect. There is no reason to think he would not go into the cave again.

    D **Correct. The passage hints that the photographs made people believe Jim White, and they became interested in Carlsbad Cavern.**

17. A **Correct. The writer describes the park as amazing and wonderful.**

    B Incorrect. The author does not mention this.

    C Incorrect. The author does not call attention to dangers.

    D Incorrect. The author never says that bats and caves are not scary.

18. A Incorrect. *Im-* added to *proper* does not mean "very proper."

    B Incorrect. *Im-* added to *proper* does not mean "slightly proper."

    C Incorrect. *Im-* added to *proper* does not mean "proper again."

    D **Correct. *Im-* added to *proper* means "not proper." *Proper* means "polite, correct, or OK." *Im-* means "not."**

19. A Incorrect. It does not refer to the sentence that includes *chilly*.

    B Incorrect. It does not refer to the sentence that includes *chilly*.

    C Incorrect. It does not refer to the sentence that includes *chilly*.

    D **Correct. It is part of the sentence that follows and relates to *chilly*.**

20. A Incorrect. The comparison is not about seeing your reflection.

    B Incorrect. The comparison is not about smoothness.

    C **Correct. The paragraph compares the lake to glass because they both are clear.**

    D Incorrect. A lake cannot be broken.

Before You Begin

Step 3 is the third step in the three-step approach and covers pages 169–251 in the student book. At Step 3 the readability and instruction are on-level, passages are longer and more challenging, and reading material is high interest. Step 3 expands on tools and vocabulary taught in Steps 1 and 2 and introduces additional strategies students can use to break down texts. Use the Student Skill Progress Chart on pages 116–117 to track each student's progress. The Skills and Items Correlation on page 118 will help identify which questions in the unit and step reviews test each skill.

Introduction to Step 3

The introduction focuses on strategies students will use in the step. Ensuring students are comfortable with these strategies before they begin skill instruction on page 174 in the student book will allow them to focus on expanding their knowledge and abilities with the skills.

Student page 170 ▶ **About Take Notes**

Explain that taking notes is writing words, ideas, and questions about what you are reading.
- Ask a volunteer to read the bulleted list for Take Notes.
- Point out the note in the margin of the passage. Then ask students to read the passage and take notes. Regroup as a class and have students share the notes they wrote.

Number the Paragraphs

Students will learn to number paragraphs to help them find information quickly.
- Say *Some questions will ask about information found in a certain paragraph. The numbers next to the paragraphs will help you find the paragraph quickly.*
- Ask students to read "The Parade," number the paragraphs, and answer Question 1. (1. B)

Student page 171 ▶ **Frame a Paragraph**

Students will learn to frame paragraphs that questions refer to so they can find them quickly.
- Show an example, such as a picture frame. Say *The picture frame goes around the picture. When you frame a paragraph, you are drawing a frame around it.*
- As a class, reread Question 1 and decide which paragraph to frame. Demonstrate placing a box around paragraph 3. Have students explain their answer choices.

Reading All the Answer Choices

Students will read all the answers to help them find the best answer choice.
- Direct students to Question 1. Ask *What are we looking for?* (parties Laura hasn't had in the past) *What are some choices?* (boating, art museum, roller skating, and swimming)
- Have pairs of students read "A Special Party" and answer the question. (1. A)

Student page 172 ▶ **Cross Out Incorrect Answers**

Students will cross out answer choices that they know are incorrect.
- Explain that by crossing out the answer choices they know are incorrect, choosing the correct answer will be easier. They can then reread the answer choices if necessary.
- Ask students to answer Question 2 and cross out the incorrect answers. (2. C)

Write the Paragraph Number Where an Answer Can Be Found

Students will write the paragraph number next to a question to help them check their work.
- Ask students to reread the passage and answer the next question.
- Regroup and have students share their answers. (paragraph 1) Redirect as necessary.

Check Your Answer

Students will learn to check their answers to be sure they answered all questions correctly.
- Say *To check that you chose the right answer, reread the question and answers and look back at the paragraph.* Ask students to check their answers for the questions on pages 170–172.

Unit 1: Comprehension

Student page 173 ▶ ### Introducing the Unit

Main idea and supporting details
Sequence
Compare and contrast
Cause and effect

Refer students to the skills listed in the box. Invite volunteers to explain what the skills mean. Help students practice the skills taught in this unit by asking the following questions. Then discuss how the comprehension skill is used in each example.

- Say *Amelia has a set of paints and three nice paintbrushes. She paints each day after school. She has painted many beautiful paintings. What is the main idea of this passage?* Have volunteers share their responses.
- Say *Mara put water in the pan and turned on the stove. Once the water was boiling, she added the noodles. Then she drained the water and added the sauce. What did Mara do first?* Have volunteers share their responses.
- Say *The van is comfortable and seats seven people. The car is comfortable but seats only four people. How are the two vehicles similar? How are they different?* Have volunteers share their responses.
- Say *Theresa left her glass of iced tea outside in the hot sun. Soon the ice in her glass melted. What caused the ice in her glass to melt?* Have volunteers share their responses.

Remind students that they will work more with these skills in the unit. Explain that at the end of the unit they will have an opportunity to do a personal evaluation of what they have learned.

At the End of the Unit

When students finish the skills in this unit, have them return to this page and complete the exercise at the bottom of the page. In this activity, your students will reflect on the following three things:

- what they learned
- what they feel good about
- what they feel they need more practice with

This exercise makes learning personal and allows students to reflect on what they've learned. Ask students to be active learners. Help them understand that they are responsible for their own learning.

Objective
To use the skills and tools learned in Steps 1 and 2 and the tools learned in the beginning of Step 3 to answer main idea and supporting details questions independently.

Student page 174 ▶ **Review the Skill**

Students review how to find the main idea and supporting details.
- Remind students that it is important to identify the supporting details in a passage.
- Give an example of the main idea and supporting details in a passage. Example: *My mom tells me it is important to eat healthy food at each meal. For breakfast I eat a banana and a bowl of cereal. At lunch I eat a ham sandwich and an apple. For dinner my mom makes me chicken and green beans. The main thing is to eat healthy meals to keep me healthy.*

Check Back
Have students review signal words on page 90.

▶ **Apply What You've Learned**

Have students review and use tools that will help them identify and answer questions about the main idea and supporting details.
- Direct students to Before You Read the Passage. Ask a volunteer to read the instructions aloud and have students complete the activity.
- Direct students to As You Read the Passage. Ask a volunteer to read the instructions aloud and have students complete the activity.
- After students finish reading the passage, direct them to After You Read the Passage. Have them complete the activity.

Student page 176 ▶ **Discuss with a Partner**

Answers
1. B, paragraph 1
2. C, paragraph 2
3. D, paragraph 4
4. C, paragraph 3

- Have pairs of students share their answers to the questions about the passage and explain their thinking to each other and then with the class.
- Direct students to Discuss with a Partner and have them answer the questions and discuss their answers.
- Regroup as a class and have students share their answers with the class.

Reteach
If students are having difficulty with the main idea and supporting details, have them do the following activity. Write these sentences on the board. *My sister helps me with my homework. She has brown hair. My big sister helps when I make my bed, too.*
- Read the sentences aloud to students. Then have students draw pictures to illustrate each sentence. Have volunteers say which pictures illustrate supporting details and then have a volunteer tell the main idea of the sentences.
- Invite students to generate their own examples and repeat the exercise.

Objective

To use the skills and tools learned in Steps 1 and 2 and the tools learned in the beginning of Step 3 to answer sequence questions independently.

Student page 177

Check Back
Have students review signal words on page 93.

▶ **Review the Skill**

Students review how to identify sequence.

- Remind students that sequence is the order in which events or steps occur.
- Give an example and ask students to identify the sequence. Example: *When doing laundry, first I sort the whites into one pile and the colors into another pile. Then I put one pile in the washer. Next I add one cup of detergent. Then I turn the washer on. Finally the laundry is washed and ready to dry.*

Apply What You've Learned

Have students review and use tools that will help them identify and answer questions about sequence.

- Direct students to Before You Read the Passage. Ask a volunteer to read the instructions aloud and have students complete the activity.
- Direct students to As You Read the Passage. Ask a volunteer to read the instructions aloud and have students complete the activity.
- After students finish reading the passage, direct them to After You Read the Passage. Have them complete the activity. (signal words in the article: *after, then, before, first, next, last*)

Student page 179

Answers

1. A, paragraph 2 of article
2. C, paragraph 3 of article
3. C, paragraph 1 of instructions
4. B, paragraph 3 of article

▶ **Discuss with a Partner**

- Have pairs of students share their answers to the questions about the passage and explain their thinking to each other and then with the class.
- Direct students to Discuss with a Partner and have them answer the questions and discuss their answers.
- Regroup as a class and have students share their answers with the class.

Reteach

If students are having difficulty with sequence, have them do the following activity. Write these sentences on the board. *I cut the apple into slices. I peeled the apple. I spread peanut butter on the apple slices.*

- Read the sentences aloud to students. Then have volunteers say which step comes first. Repeat for steps 2 and 3.
- Have students draw pictures that illustrate the steps in the correct order. Then have them create their own step-by-step illustrations for a daily task. Classmates can practice putting each other's illustrations in the correct sequence.

Step 3　Skill 3 ■ Compare and Contrast

Objective
To use the skills and tools learned in Steps 1 and 2 and the test tools learned in the beginning of Step 3 to answer compare and contrast questions independently.

Student page 180 ▶ **Review the Skill**

Students review how to identify compare and contrast.
- Remind students that to compare is to find ways in which two or more things are alike, and to contrast is to find ways in which they are different.
- Give examples and ask students to compare and contrast. Example: *cats and dogs* (both pets, both have tails, cats meow, dogs bark) or *cars and bicycles* (both have wheels, different number of wheels, cars need gas).

Check Back

Have students review signal words on page 96.

▶ **Apply What You've Learned**

Have students review and use tools that will help them identify and answer questions about compare and contrast.
- Direct students to Before You Read the Passage. Ask a volunteer to read the instructions aloud and have students complete the activity.
- Direct students to As You Read the Passage. Ask a volunteer to read the instructions aloud and have students complete the activity.
- After students finish reading the passage, direct them to After You Read the Passage. Have them complete the activity. (signal words in the passage: *alike, although, different, just as, but, while, on the other hand, however, both, like, though*)

Student page 182 ▶ **Discuss with a Partner**
- Have pairs of students share their answers to the questions about the passage and explain their thinking to each other and then to the class.
- Direct students to Discuss with a Partner and have them answer the questions and discuss their answers.
- Regroup as a class and have students share their answers with the class.

Answers
1. C, paragraph 6
2. A, paragraph 3
3. A, paragraph 5
4. B, paragraph 6

Reteach
If students are having difficulty with compare and contrast, have them do the following activity. Write these sentences on the board. *Both planes and boats are ways to travel. Planes fly, but boats float.*
- Have students identify the signal words. (*both, but*) Using the signal words from page 96, have students rewrite the sentences using different signal words. Example: *Planes, as well as boats, are ways to travel. However, planes fly, while boats float.*
- Write the new sentences on the board. Redirect as necessary. Then have students generate their own sentences and repeat the activity.

Objective

To use the skills and tools learned in Steps 1 and 2 and the tools learned in the beginning of Step 3 to answer cause and effect questions independently.

Student page 183 ▶ **Review the Skill**

Students review how to find cause and effect.

Check Back

Have students review signal words on page 99.

- Remind students that effect is what happens and cause is why something happens.
- Give examples and ask students to identify cause and effect. Example: *I slipped on the banana peel* (effect) *because I didn't see it* (cause).

Apply What You've Learned

Have students review and use tools that will help them identify and answer questions about cause and effect.

- Direct students to Before You Read the Passage. Ask a volunteer to read the instructions aloud and have students complete the activity.
- Direct students to As You Read the Passage. Ask a volunteer to read the instructions aloud and have students complete the activity.
- After students finish reading the passage, direct them to After You Read the Passage. Have them complete the activity. (signal words in passage: *so, so that, because, as a result*)

Student page 185 ▶ **Discuss with a Partner**

Answers

1. B, paragraph 1
2. D, paragraph 4
3. D, paragraph 5
4. A, paragraph 6

- Have pairs of students share their answers to the questions about the passage and explain their thinking to each other and then with the class.
- Direct students to Discuss with a Partner and have them answer the questions and discuss their answers.
- Regroup as a class and have students share their answers with the class.

Reteach

If students are having difficulty with cause and effect, have them do the following activity. Write these sentences on the board. *I didn't go swimming. The water was too cold.*

- Have students write the signal words from page 99 on separate 3 × 5 cards. Have them write *cause, effect, The water was too cold,* and *I didn't go swimming* on separate 3 × 5 cards. Have students arrange the cards to make different sentences showing cause and effect. Then have them put the cause card above the cause and the effect card above the effect.
- Invite students to generate their own sentences and repeat the exercise.

effect		cause
I didn't go swimming.	because	The water was too cold.

Answers

Something to Cheer About

1. A Incorrect. Noura is going to sleep in, but that does not mean she is lazy.
   B Incorrect. Noura seems to enjoy staying indoors.
   C Incorrect. Noura plans to sleep in, but that is because she does not like winter.
   D **Correct. Noura makes the statement that she does not like winter.**

2. A Incorrect. Noura plays games with her friends *after* the snow begins to fall.
   B **Correct. This is the correct order of events.**
   C Incorrect. Noura has breakfast first, *before* the snow begins to fall.
   D Incorrect. Noura has breakfast *before* both of the other events.

3. A **Correct. The snow kept falling and prevented them from getting home.**
   B Incorrect. This is not mentioned in the passage.
   C Incorrect. The snow, not the cold, kept them at school.
   D Incorrect. This is not mentioned in the passage.

4. A Incorrect. Noura does not like winter.
   B **Correct. These are all true.**
   C Incorrect. This answer shows how they are alike, not different.
   D Incorrect. This answer shows how they are alike, not different.

5. A Incorrect. Noura is briefly outside in the snow with her friends, but she does not have fun.
   B Incorrect. Noura never tries or watches any of these sports.
   C **Correct. The events of the story lead up to this main idea.**
   D Incorrect. Noura changes her mind because she has fun during the early vacation, not because her friends changed her mind.

Unit 2: Fiction and Nonfiction Skills

Student page 188 ▶ **Introducing the Unit**

Refer students to the skills listed in the box. Invite volunteers to explain what the skills mean. Help students practice the skills taught in this unit by doing the following activity. Read each passage and question below aloud, then invite students to offer answers. Discuss how each situation relates to a fiction or nonfiction skill.

Character
Plot and setting
Theme
Literary elements
Structural elements
Visual information
Nonfiction writing

1. *Cliff woke up and went swimming. Then he rode his bike. After that he did fifty push-ups. What type of person is Cliff?* (energetic)
2. *It was autumn, and Clara was at her grandmother's cottage in the woods. While taking a hike to look for flowers, Clara got lost in the forest. What is the plot?* (Clara gets lost) *What is the setting?* (cottage and forest)
3. *Harry was nervous about his test. His brother helped him study and told Harry that he knew Harry would do well. This made Harry feel better and study harder. Harry got an A on his test. What is the theme?* (work hard to achieve goals)
4. *Because he was not allowed to move, the castle guard was a statue. What literary element is this?* (metaphor)
5. *Felix was not sure which chapter to read first, so he looked at the table of contents. Then he looked at the index. What skill was Felix using?* (structural elements)
6. *When Gina read the article about skyscrapers, she studied the chart that showed the world's tallest buildings and their heights. What skill did Gina use?* (visual information)
7. *Kwan enjoyed the biography of baseball player Jackie Robinson. What type of writing is the biography?* (nonfiction writing)

At the End of the Unit

When students finish the skills in this unit, have them return to this page and complete the exercise at the bottom of the page. In this activity, your students will reflect on the following three things:

- what they learned
- what they feel good about
- what they feel they need more practice with

This exercise makes learning personal and allows students to reflect on what they've learned. Ask students to be active learners. Help them understand that they are responsible for their own learning.

Objective

To use the skills and tools learned in Steps 1 and 2 and the tools learned at the beginning of Step 3 to answer character questions independently.

Student page 189

Check Back

Have students review signal words on page 105.

▶ **Review the Skill**

Students review how to find clues to help identify character traits.

- Remind students that a character is a person, animal, or make-believe creature in a story. Each passage contains clues that show what the characters are like.
- Give examples and ask students to tell you about the character. Example: *Marla followed her mother into the kitchen and began to put away groceries.* Ask *What kind of person is Marla?* (helpful, thoughtful)

▶ **Apply What You've Learned**

Have students review and use tools that will help them identify and answer questions about characters.

- Direct students to Before You Read the Passage. Ask a volunteer to read the instructions aloud and have students complete the activity.
- Direct students to As You Read the Passage. Ask a volunteer to read the instructions aloud and have the students complete the activity.
- After students finish reading the passage, direct them to After You Read the Passage. Have them complete the activity.

Student page 191

Answers

1. B, paragraph 3
2. A, paragraph 5
3. C
4. A, paragraph 7

▶ **Discuss with a Partner**

- Have pairs of students share their answers to the questions about the passage and explain their thinking to each other and then with the class.
- Direct students to Discuss with a Partner and have them answer the questions and discuss their answers.
- Regroup as a class and have students share their answers with the class.

Reteach

If students are having difficulty with characters, have them do the following activity.

- Write the following sentences on the board.
  "I am too busy to help you," Eduardo said. "Let me help you with that," Sarah said. Sarah picked up the box and carried it inside. Eduardo turned away and went back to his work.
- Have students write each sentence on a separate 3 × 5 card. Then have students separate the sentences into those that likely describe Eduardo and those that likely describe Sarah. Then ask students to name a word that describes both characters, based on their actions and words.
- Invite students to generate their own sentences and repeat the exercise.

Character 1	Character 2
"I am too busy to help you," Eduardo said.	"Let me help you with that," Sarah said.
Eduardo turned away and went back to his work.	Sarah picked up the box and carried it inside.

Objective

To use the skills and tools learned in Steps 1 and 2 and the tools learned at the beginning of Step 3 to answer plot and setting questions independently.

Student page 192

Check Back

Have students review signal words on page 108.

▶ Review the Skill

Students review how to find plot and setting.

- Remind students that the plot is the events or action in a story, and the setting is where and when a story takes place.
- Give examples and ask students to identify plot and setting. Example: *Alex shot the basketball right into the net.* Ask *Where is Alex?* (on a basketball court) Ask *What happens in this sentence?* (Alex scores in basketball.)

▶ Apply What You've Learned

Have students review and use tools that will help them identify and answer questions about plot and setting.

- Direct students to Before You Read the Passage. Ask a volunteer to read the instructions aloud and have students complete the activity.
- Direct students to As You Read the Passage. Ask a volunteer to read the instructions aloud and have students complete the activity.
- After students finish reading the passage, direct them to After You Read the Passage. Have them complete the activity.

Student page 194

Answers

1. B, paragraph 12
2. A, paragraph 1
3. C, throughout passage
4. D, paragraph 1

▶ Discuss with a Partner

- Have pairs of students share their answers to the questions about the passage and explain their thinking to each other and then with the class.
- Direct students to Discuss with a Partner and have them answer the questions and discuss their answers.
- Regroup as a class and have students share their answers with the class.

Reteach

If students are having difficulty with plot and setting, have them do the following activity.

- Have students write the words *action/plot* and *setting* on separate 3 × 5 cards. Have them write each of the following sentences on separate 3 × 5 cards: *She took out a shovel and began to dig. Instead, she found a rusty nail. But no treasure was buried in the yard.* Have students arrange the sentences to make a story. Then have students put the sentences that tell about actions under the *action/plot* card and the sentences that tell about where and when the action takes place under the *setting* card.
- Invite students to generate their own sentences and repeat the exercise.

action/plot	setting
She took out a shovel and began to dig.	But no treasure was buried in the yard.
Instead, she found a rusty nail.	

Objective
To use the skills and tools learned in Steps 1 and 2 and the tools learned in the beginning of Step 3 to answer questions about theme independently.

Student page 195 ▶ **Review the Skill**

Students review how to identify the theme of a passage.
- Remind students that the theme is a message that the author is trying to tell you about life.
- Read a short children's book and ask students to identify the theme.

Check Back

Have students review the common themes on page 111.

Apply What You've Learned
Have students review and use tools that will help them identify and answer questions about theme.
- Direct students to Before You Read the Passage. Ask a volunteer to read the instructions aloud and have students complete the activity.
- Direct students to As You Read the Passage. Ask a volunteer to read the instructions aloud and have students complete the activity.
- After students finish reading the passage, direct them to After You Read the Passage. Have them complete the activity.

Student page 197 ▶ **Discuss with a Partner**

Answers
1. A, paragraph 33
2. D, paragraph 14
3. B, paragraphs 18–24
4. B, paragraph 13

- Pair students and invite them to share their answers to the questions about the passage. Have them explain their thinking to each other and then with the class.
- Direct students to Discuss with a Partner and have them answer the questions and discuss their answers.
- Regroup as a class and have students share their answers with the class.

Reteach
For students having difficulty identifying the theme, have them do the following activity.
- On the board, write a short version of a fable, such as "The Boy Who Cried Wolf."
- Have students identify the lesson the boy learns.
- Invite students to draw and fill in a theme chart on the board, writing the theme of the fable in their own words.

Objective
To use the skills and tools learned in Steps 1 and 2 and the tools learned in the beginning of Step 3 to answer questions about literary elements independently.

Student page 198 ▶ ## Review the Skill
Students review how to find literary elements.
- Remind students that literary elements are used in stories and poems to create pictures or ideas in the reader's mind.
- Give examples and ask students to identify the literary elements. Example: *The wind was so strong on top of the hill, it made my eyes water like a faucet.*

Check Back

Have students review the signal words on page 114.

Apply What You've Learned
Have students review and use tools that will help them identify and answer questions about literary elements.
- Direct students to Before You Read the Passage. Ask a volunteer to read the instructions aloud and have students complete the activity.
- Direct students to As You Read the Passage. Ask a volunteer to read the instructions aloud and have students complete the activity.
- After students finish reading the passage, direct them to After You Read the Passage. Have them complete the activity.

Literary elements in passage:
- paragraph 2: similes: mother was alert as a raven, hair like feathers, aunts like hens in a henhouse; metaphor: dress was a shimmering rainbow
- paragraph 6: simile: words flowed like liquid, moon like a grandmother

Student page 200 ▶ ## Discuss with a Partner
- Have pairs of students share their answers to the questions about the passage. Have them explain their thinking to each other and then to the class.
- Direct students to Discuss with a Partner and have them answer the questions and discuss their answers.
- Regroup as a class and have students share their answers with the class.

Answers
1. A, paragraph 2
2. B, paragraph 2
3. D, paragraph 6
4. B, paragraph 6

Reteach
If students are having difficulty with literary elements, have them do the following activity. As a class, compose a poem. Have students include at least one simile and one metaphor in the poem. Choose a subject that is familiar to students, such as technology, space, or music.

Objective

To use the skills and tools learned in Steps 1 and 2 and the tools learned in the beginning of Step 3 to answer structural elements questions independently.

Student page 201 ▶ **Review the Skill**

Students review the key parts of a book.

- Remind students that knowing the parts of a book can help you understand what you read.
- Give examples and ask students what the headings might be telling the reader. Examples: *Beach Fun, Ways to Relax, Things Friends Do.*
- Ask students to give specific examples of the types of activities that might be included under each heading.

Check Back

Have students review signal words on page 117.

▶ **Apply What You've Learned**

Have students review and use tools that will help them identify and answer questions about structural elements.

- Direct students to Before You Read the Passage. Ask a volunteer to read the instructions aloud and have students complete the activity.
- Direct students to As You Read the Passage and ask a volunteer to read the instructions aloud. Have students complete the activity.
- After students finish reading the passage, direct them to After You Read the Passage. Have them complete the activity.

Student page 203 ▶ **Discuss with a Partner**

- Have pairs of students share their answers to the questions about the passage and explain their thinking to each other and then with the class.
- Direct students to Discuss with a Partner and have them answer the questions and discuss their answers.
- Regroup as a class and have students share their answers with the class.

Answers

1. A, paragraph 4
2. B
3. A, paragraph 7
4. B

Reteach

If students are having difficulty with structural elements, have them do the following activity. Write a subhead or title on a card. On other cards, write topics that would fall under each of the subheads or titles. For example, a title card might include the title *Team Sports* or *Animals That Live in Water.* A topics card might include *soccer, basketball, baseball* or *dolphins, sharks, crabs.* Ask students to match the title card with the correct topics card.

Objective
To use the skills and tools learned in Steps 1 and 2 and the tools learned in the beginning of Step 3 to answer visual information questions independently.

Student page 204 ▶ ### Review the Skill
Students review the importance of looking at and reviewing graphics to find information that may not be included in a passage.
- Remind students that visual information helps them understand the meaning of numbers and facts.

<table>
<tr><td>

Check Back

Have students review key words on page 120.

</td></tr>
</table>

▶ ### Apply What You've Learned
Have students review and use tools that will help them identify and answer questions about visual information.
- Direct students to Before You Read the Passage. Ask a volunteer to read the instructions aloud and have students complete the activity.
- Direct students to As You Read the Passage. Ask a volunteer to read the instructions aloud and have students complete the activity.
- After students finish reading the passage, direct them to After You Read the Passage. Have them complete the activity. (key words in passage: *picture, map*)

Student page 206 ▶ ### Discuss with a Partner

Answers
1. B, map
2. A, map
3. D, paragraph 1
4. B, paragraph 3

- Have pairs of students share their answers to the questions about the passage. Have them explain their thinking to each other and then to the class.
- Direct students to Discuss with a Partner and have them answer the questions and discuss their answers.
- Regroup as a class and have students share their answers with the class.

Reteach
If students are having difficulty with visual information, have them do the following activity.
- Cut charts and graphs apart and discuss each component.
- Have students read photo captions aloud and discuss their meaning.
- Invite students to create a chart of the lunch selections at school today and how many students chose each.

Objective
To use the skills and tools learned in Steps 1 and 2 and the tools learned in the beginning of Step 3 to answer nonfiction writing questions independently.

Student page 207

Check Back

Have students review signal words on page 123.

▶ Review the Skill
Students review how to identify the types of nonfiction writing.
- Remind students that a biography is a true life story, persuasive writing tries to convince the reader to think or act in a certain way, functional writing gives step-by-step instructions, and informative writing gives information and facts.
- Give examples and ask students to identify each type of writing. Example: *Bats are nocturnal creatures.* (informative)

▶ Apply What You've Learned
Have students review and use tools that will help them identify and answer questions about the types of nonfiction writing.
- Direct students to Before You Read the Passage. Ask a volunteer to read the instructions aloud and have students complete the activity.
- Direct students to As You Read the Passage. Ask a volunteer to read the instructions aloud and have students complete the activity.
- After students finish reading the passage, direct them to After You Read the Passage. Have them complete the activity.

Student page 209

Answers
1. C, entire passage
2. C
3. B, entire passage
4. C, paragraph 7

▶ Discuss with a Partner
- Have pairs of students share their answers to the questions about the passage and explain their thinking to each other and then with the class.
- Direct students to Discuss with a Partner and have them answer the questions and discuss their answers.
- Regroup as a class and have students share their answers with the class.

▶ Reteach
If students are having difficulty with types of nonfiction writing, have them do the following activity.
- Write the following sentences on the board as models for the types of nonfiction writing.
  First read the directions, then gather your materials.
  I think that Crispy Crunch cereal is the best kind of cereal.
  This great composer was born on July 4, 1809.
  Dolphins and whales are mammals, not fish.
- Make sure students understand the type of nonfiction writing represented by each sentence. (functional, persuasive, biographical, informative)
- Help students create sentences of their own, modeled after the ones on the board.
- Invite students to write additional sentences on their own and then share them with a partner.

Answers

A World of Trees

1. A   Incorrect. It does not report the news.
   B   Incorrect. It tells facts, not made-up events.
   C   **Correct. It gives facts and information about a topic.**
   D   Incorrect. It is not a story about someone's life.

2. A   Incorrect. The information covers both hardwood and softwood trees.
   B   **Correct. This heading indicates information about types of trees.**
   C   Incorrect. The information covers both hardwood and softwood trees.
   D   Incorrect. The information in the passage is about more than seeds and fruits.

3. A   Incorrect. According to the diagram, the bud does not connect the leaf blade to the stem.
   B   Incorrect. The vein is part of the leaf.
   C   Incorrect. The midvein is part of the leaf.
   D   **Correct. According to the diagram, the stalk connects the leaf blade to the stem.**

A New Life

4. A   Incorrect. Nothing in the passage suggests Lupe is angry.
   B   **Correct. Lupe misses her sister and hopes a girl her age will move in.**
   C   Incorrect. Lupe is not described as being rude.
   D   Incorrect. Nothing in the passage suggests Lupe is humble.

5. A   Incorrect. She has not met anyone when the story ends.
   B   Incorrect. This happens at the beginning of the story.
   C   Incorrect. This has already happened before the story begins.
   D   **Correct. This is the last event in the story.**

6. A   **Correct. The theme throughout the passage indicates the importance of having friends of one's own age.**
   B   Incorrect. Nothing in the passage suggests standing up for beliefs.
   C   Incorrect. The passage does not deal with honesty versus lying.
   D   Incorrect. Although the passage addresses the need for friendship, trust in a friendship is not addressed.

7. A   Incorrect. A toy that is abandoned is probably not well-liked by children, so this is not the reason for the comparison.
   B   **Correct. Lupe feels like she is abandoned, much like a toy that isn't played with is also abandoned.**
   C   Incorrect. A toy that is not played with is probably no longer fun to play with. This is not the reason for the comparison.
   D   Incorrect. Not all toys stay in an apartment building. This is not the reason for the comparison.

Unit 3: Vocabulary

Student page 212 ▶

Root words, prefixes, and suffixes
Synonyms and antonyms
Context clues
Multiple-meaning words

Introducing the Unit

Refer students to the skills listed in the box. Review the skills by having students define or explain each one.

Help students work with the vocabulary skills by doing the exercises described below. Have students work in pairs to complete each task.

1. *Make a list of all the prefixes you can think of.*
2. *Make a list of all the suffixes you can think of.*
3. *Think of a root word that both a prefix and a suffix can be added to.*
4. *Write down as many different synonyms and antonyms as you can think of for the word small.*
5. *Write down as many different synonyms and antonyms as you can think of for the word good.*
6. Say *Read the sentence I will write on the board. Try to use context clues to learn the meaning of the unfamiliar word.* Write this sentence on the board: underline the word *spacious. She loved the spacious room because she could fill it with many things.*
7. Say *Read the sentence I will write on the board. Try to use context clues to learn the meaning of the unfamiliar word.* Write this sentence on the board. *The inquisitive boy never stopped asking questions.* Then underline the word *inquisitive.*
8. *List at least two different meanings of the word* set.
9. *Find as many meanings as you can for each of these words:* check, flare, plot, ram, *and* sink.

At the End of the Unit

When students finish the skills in this unit, have them return to this page. Then have them complete the exercise at the bottom of the page. In this activity, your students will reflect on the following three things:

- what they learned
- what they feel good about
- what they feel they need more practice with

This exercise makes learning personal and allows students to reflect on what they've learned. Ask students to be active learners. Help them understand that they are responsible for their own learning.

Objective

To use the skills and tools learned in Steps 1 and 2 and the tools learned in the beginning of Step 3 to understand vocabulary by identifying root words, prefixes, and suffixes and associating them with their meanings.

Student page 213 ▶ ## Review the Skill

Students review how to identify root words, prefixes, and suffixes.

Check Back

Have students review root words, prefixes, and suffixes on page 129.

- Remind students that a root word is the base of a word. A prefix is a word part that comes before a root word and changes its meaning. A suffix is a word part that comes after a root word and changes its meaning.
- Write the following on the board:

  un-   re-   success   place   -ful   -able

- Have students identify the prefixes (*un-, re-*), root words (*success, place*), and suffixes (*-ful, -able*). Ask them for the meaning of each. Then have them combine the elements to form words and have them read the words aloud. (*unsuccessful, replaceable*)

▶ ## Apply What You've Learned

Have students review and use tools that will help them identify root words, prefixes, suffixes, and word meanings.

- Direct students to Before You Read the Passage. Ask a volunteer to read the instructions aloud and have students complete the activity.
- Direct students to As You Read the Passage. Ask a volunteer to read the instructions aloud and have students complete the activity. (*un-, aware, not aware; dis-, similar, not similar; un-, detect, -able, not able to be detected; un-, explain, -able, not able to be explained*)
- After students finish reading the passage, direct them to After You Read the Passage. Have them complete the activity.

Student page 215 ▶ ## Discuss with a Partner

Answers

1. C, paragraph 1
2. B, paragraph 3
3. A, paragraph 5
4. B, paragraph 3

- Pair students and invite them to share their answers to the questions about the passage. Have them explain their thinking to each other and then to the class.
- Direct students to Discuss with a Partner and have them answer the questions and discuss their answers.
- Regroup as a class and have students share their answers with the class.

Reteach

If students are having difficulty with root words, have them do the following activity.

- Create index cards with prefixes, root words, and suffixes on separate cards. Write the prefix, root word, or suffix on the front of the card and its definition on the back.
- Have students make words with the cards that include prefixes, suffixes, or both. Direct students to write what they think the word means and to use it in a sentence.
- Put students in groups and have them check their lists with each other.

Objective
To use the skills and tools learned in Steps 1 and 2 and the tools learned in the beginning of Step 3 to answer questions about synonyms and antonyms.

Student page 216 ▶ **Review the Skill**

Students review how to identify synonyms and antonyms.

- Remind students that synonyms are words that have similar meanings (bitter, sour). Antonyms are words that have opposite meanings (weak, strong).
- Remind students to look for a nearby synonym or antonym as a clue to the meaning of an unfamiliar word.

Check Back
Have students review examples of synonym and antonym signal words on page 132.

Synonyms
safe – secure
Antonyms
recognized – unknown
deluge – light rain
substantial – thin

▶ **Apply What You've Learned**

Have students review and use tools that will help them identify synonyms and antonyms.

- Direct students to Before You Read the Passage and ask a volunteer to read the instructions aloud. Have students complete the activity. (signal words in questions: 1. *antonym* 4. *synonym*)
- Direct students to As You Read the Passage and ask a volunteer to read the instructions aloud. Have students complete the activity.
- After students finish reading the passage, direct them to After You Read the Passage. Have them complete the activity.

Student page 218 ▶ **Discuss with a Partner**

- Pair students and invite them to share their answers to the questions about the passage. Have them explain their thinking to each other and then to the class.
- Direct students to the box at the bottom of the page and have them answer the questions and discuss their answers.
- Regroup as a class and have students share their answers with the class.

Answers
1. C, paragraph 1
2. B, paragraph 4
3. C, paragraph 6
4. D, paragraph 5

Reteach
For students who are having difficulty with synonyms and antonyms, do the following activity.

- Write the heading *Same* on the board. Suggest a number of words for which there are synonyms and ask students to name words that mean the same thing. Write the synonym pairs on the board. Remind students that words that have similar meanings are called synonyms. Examples: *small, little; pretty, lovely; big, large; loud, noisy; quiet, silent.*
- Write the heading *Different* on the board. Follow the same procedure, having students give antonyms for words you name. Write the antonym pairs on the board. Remind students that words that have opposite meanings are called antonyms. Examples: *small, large; friend, enemy; loud, soft; quiet, noisy; up, down.*
- Ask students to choose pairs of synonyms or antonyms to use in sentences. Redirect as necessary.

Objective

To use the skills and tools learned in Steps 1 and 2 and the tools learned in the beginning of Step 3 to answer context clues questions independently.

Student page 219 ▶ **Review the Skill**

Students review how to use context clues to decipher new words.

Check Back

Have students review the types of context clues on page 135.

- Remind students that context clues can be found in the words or sentences around an unfamiliar word and can help them define a new word.
- Give examples and ask students to identify the context clues. Example: *It is smart to wear a warm coat* (context clue) *such as a* parka (unfamiliar word) *to go out in a snowstorm.*

▶ **Apply What You've Learned**

Have students review and use tools that will help them identify context clues and decipher the meaning of unfamiliar words.

- Direct students to Before You Read the Passage. Ask a volunteer to read the instructions aloud and have students complete the activity.
- Direct students to As You Read the Passage. Ask a volunteer to read the instructions aloud and have students complete the activity. (context clues in passage: *pod–this shell; lack–not enough; underneath–lying in the shadows; credit–deserve the praise*)
- After students finish reading the passage, direct them to After You Read the Passage. Have them complete the activity.

Student page 221 ▶ **Discuss with a Partner**

Answers

1. B, paragraph 1
2. C, paragraph 3
3. C, paragraph 4
4. B, paragraph 7

- Have pairs of students share their answers to the questions about the passage and explain their thinking to each other and then to the class.
- Direct students to Discuss with a Partner and have them answer the questions and discuss their answers.
- Regroup as a class and have students share their answers with the class.

Reteach

If students are having difficulty with context clues, have them do the following activity.

- Write this sentence on the board.
  If I need to eat between meals, a healthy snack such as apples and peanut butter helps me feel better than a sugary treat would.
- Write *snack* on a piece of colored paper. Then write *eat between meals* on an inflated balloon. Also write *apples and peanut butter* and *treat* on balloons. Have a volunteer hold up the colored paper, and have three others stand around him, each holding one of the balloons. Say *The context clues on the balloons help you understand the meaning of* snack *in the sentence on the board.*
- Then have students work in groups to generate their own sentences and repeat the activity. Redirect as necessary.

Objective

To use the skills and tools learned in Steps 1 and 2 and the tools learned in the beginning of Step 3 to answer multiple-meaning word questions independently.

Student page 222 ▶ **Review the Skill**

Check Back

Have students review the signal words on page 138.

Students review how to identify multiple-meaning words and how to try different meanings for words that don't make sense.

- Remind students that multiple-meaning words have several meanings depending on how they are used in a sentence.
- Give examples and ask students to identify the different meanings for the multiple-meaning word. Example: *The* root *of the plant is long.* (the part of a plant that grows beneath the ground) *The* root *of the fight was a missing book.* (cause)

▶ **Apply What You've Learned**

Have students review and use tools that will help them identify multiple-meaning words and decide which meaning is correct.

- Direct students to Before You Read the Passage. Ask a volunteer to read the instructions aloud and have students complete the activity.
- Direct students to As You Read the Passage. Ask a volunteer to read the instructions aloud and have students complete the activity.
- After students finish reading the passage, direct them to After You Read the Passage. Have them complete the activity.

Student page 224 ▶ **Discuss with a Partner**

Answers

1. D, paragraph 2
2. A, paragraph 6
3. B, paragraph 4
4. C, paragraph 5

- Have pairs of students share their answers to the questions about the passage and explain their thinking to each other and then to the class.
- Direct students to Discuss with a Partner and have them answer the questions and discuss their answers.
- Regroup as a class and have students share their answers with the class.

Reteach

If students are having difficulty with multiple-meaning words, have them do the following activity.

- Write each multiple-meaning word from this lesson on an index card with the word on the blank side. On separate cards write different definitions for each word, using one card for each definition.
- Pass out the cards to students.
- Have students find the person who has the multiple-meaning word that matches their definition. Then have students whose cards match work together to generate their own sentences for each meaning of the word.
- Invite students to take turns writing their sentences on the board. Redirect as necessary.

Answers

Sparkle's Fourth of July

1. A Incorrect. Dark skies are not a sign of a celebration, so this answer is not a context clue.

   B Correct. Fireworks are a sign of a celebration.

   C Incorrect. People sit outside for many reasons, so this answer is not a context clue.

   D Incorrect. Without more information, these words do not give a clue about the meaning of *celebration*.

2. A Incorrect. Frank is the youngest. His brother and sister are older.

   B Incorrect. The suffix *-est* tells us that he does not have a brother or sister the same age as him.

   C Incorrect. That would make Frank the oldest, not the youngest.

   D Correct. The suffix *-est* tells us that Frank is the "most" young in the family, so everyone is older than he is.

3. **A Correct. *Concerned* means "nervous," the opposite of relaxed.**

   B Incorrect. This answer has a similar meaning to *concerned* and is not an antonym.

   C Incorrect. This answer means "protected" and is not the opposite of *concerned.*

   D Incorrect. This answer has a similar meaning to *concerned* and is not an antonym.

4. A Incorrect. *Even* numbers are divisible by two. *Even* does not make sense in both sentences.

   B Incorrect. *All* is correct in the first sentence, but not in the second.

   C Correct. This answer is correct in both sentences. *Odd* can refer to numbers such as 1, 3, 5, 7, 9, etc., and it can also mean "strange" or "unusual."

   D Incorrect. *Unusual* is correct in the second sentence, but not in the first.

Unit 4: Critical Thinking

Student page 226 ▶ **Introducing the Unit**

Author's purpose
Facts and opinions
Draw conclusions
    and make
    inferences
Make predictions
Summarize

Refer students to the skills listed in the box. Invite volunteers to explain what the skills mean. Encourage students to name specific words or phrases that signal each skill.

Help students practice using the skills taught in this unit by reading aloud each passage and question below. Have volunteers share their responses with the class.

1. Say *This is how you should wash your hands. First go to the sink and turn on the water. Wet your hands. Then put some soap on your hands and rub them together. Rinse the soap off. Dry your hands.* Then ask *Why do you think the author wrote this passage?*

2. Say *I think my bedroom is great. The walls are painted blue. The light is nice and bright. The rug is brown.* Then ask *What opinions are given in this passage?*

3. Say *Alicia bought a plant. The man at the store told her to water it every day and give it lots of sunshine. When Alicia got home, she put the plant on a table and forgot about it. A few days later Alicia remembered the plant. She saw that the plant was brown and had lost many leaves.* Then ask *What conclusion can you draw about what happened to the plant?*

4. Say *Weldon was very hungry after school. He walked to the bus stop. His friend Jamal asked him to play baseball after school. Weldon agreed but then remembered his grandmother was making his favorite kind of cookies after school.* Then ask *What do you think Weldon will do?*

5. Say *Chandri got up very early. She went for a run, came home and took a shower, did some reading, and then went to school. After school, she went to soccer practice, and then she came home for dinner. After dinner, she helped clean the table, and then she did her homework.* Then ask *How would you summarize Chandri's day?*

At the End of the Unit

When students finish the skills in this unit, have them return to this page. Then have them complete the exercise at the bottom of the page. In this activity, your students will reflect on the following three things:

- what they learned
- what they feel good about
- what they feel they need more practice with

This exercise makes learning personal and allows students to reflect on what they've learned. Ask students to be active learners. Help them understand that they are responsible for their own learning.

Objective

To use the skills and tools learned in Steps 1 and 2 and the tools learned in the beginning of Step 3 to answer questions about the author's purpose independently.

Student page 227 ▶ **Review the Skill**

Students review how to find the author's purpose.

- Remind students that the author's purpose is the reason the author wrote a passage. Reasons include to persuade, to inform, to entertain, or to express feelings.

Check Back

Have students review the signal words on page 143.

▶ **Apply What You've Learned**

Have students review and use tools that will help them identify and answer questions about the author's purpose.

- Direct students to Before You Read the Passage. Ask a volunteer to read the instructions aloud and have students complete the activity.
- Direct students to As You Read the Passage. Ask a volunteer to read the instructions aloud and have students complete the activity.
- After students finish reading the passage, direct them to After You Read the Passage. Have them complete the activity. (Signal words: *You might discover, Starting a hobby like mine is easy, All you need, If you listen* Purpose: persuade you to begin collecting facts) (Another purpose: inform you about collecting facts, Signal words: *I'm a collector, My hobby started because I like to read, Interesting facts are all around us, I collect facts because*)

Student page 229 ▶ **Discuss with a Partner**

- Have pairs of students share their answers to the questions about the passage and explain their thinking to each other and then to the class.
- Direct students to Discuss with a Partner and have them answer the questions and discuss their answers.
- Regroup as a class and have students share their answers with the class.

Answers

1. A, paragraphs 1 and 6
2. C, paragraph 1
3. B, paragraph 2
4. D, paragraph 4

Reteach

If students are having difficulty with the author's purpose, have them do the following activity.

- Bring in an assortment of different types of writing from newspapers or magazines, e.g., cartoons, ads, letters to the editor. Have students read the passages and then state their purpose. Have students check each other's purpose for accuracy. Then have students explain how they came up with the purpose. For example, a cartoon is meant to be funny. Therefore, the author's purpose is to entertain.

Objective

To use the skills and tools learned in Steps 1 and 2 and the tools learned in the beginning of Step 3 to answer facts and opinions questions independently.

Student page 230 ▶ **Review the Skill**

Students review how to determine facts and opinions.

<table>
<tr><td>

Check Back

Have students review signal words on page 146.

</td></tr>
</table>

- Remind students that a fact can be proved true. It can be checked in a reference book or other sources. An opinion tells how someone feels or believes. It cannot be proved true.
- Give examples and ask students to identify facts and opinions. Example: *The movie began two hours ago.* (fact) *I think this movie is boring.* (opinion)

▶ **Apply What You've Learned**

Have students review and use tools that will help them identify and answer questions about facts and opinions.

- Direct students to Before You Read the Passage. Ask a volunteer to read the instructions aloud and have students complete the activity.
- Direct students to As You Read the Passage. Ask a volunteer to read the instructions aloud and have students complete the activity.
- After students finish reading the passage, direct them to After You Read the Passage. Have them complete the activity. (signal words in passage: *greatest, incredible, amazing, best, interesting, worst, beautiful*)

Student page 232 ▶ **Discuss with a Partner**

- Pair students and invite them to share their answers to the questions about the passage. Have them explain their thinking to each other and then to the class.
- Direct students to the box at the bottom of the page and have them answer the questions and discuss their answers.
- Regroup as a class and have students share their answers with the class.

Answers

1. A, paragraph 6
2. C, paragraph 3
3. D, paragraph 1
4. B

Reteach

If students are having difficulty with facts and opinions, have them do the following activity.

- Write the following headings on the board: *Can be proved, Cannot be proved.*
- Then read aloud the following sentence: *The sun is a star in the sky.* Ask *Can this statement be proved?* (yes) Write the sentence under *Can be proved.* Say *The sun is the most beautiful star in the sky.* Ask *Can this statement be proved?* (no) Write the sentence under *Cannot be proved.*
- Discuss with students how the facts can be proved. They might look them up in a reference book. They might observe them for themselves. Then discuss why the opinions cannot be proved. Direct them to the opinion signal words.

Objective

To use the skills and tools learned in Steps 1 and 2 and the tools learned in the beginning of Step 3 to answer draw conclusions and make inferences questions independently.

Student page 233

▶ Review the Skill

Students review how to draw conclusions and make inferences.

Check Back

Have students review examples of signal words that tell you to draw conclusions and make inferences on page 149.

- Remind students that a conclusion is an idea about a passage based on details in the passage. An inference is an idea based on what you already know plus passage details.
- Give examples and ask students to draw conclusions and make inferences. For example, *I heard a band playing and saw floats. What conclusion can you draw about what is happening?* (There is a parade.) *Fireworks exploded in the sky. The dog trembled. What inference can you make about the dog?* (The fireworks frightened the dog.)

▶ Apply What You've Learned

Have students review and use tools that will help them draw conclusions and make inferences in order to answer questions.

- Direct students to Before You Read the Passage. Ask a volunteer to read the instructions aloud and have students complete the activity. (signal words in questions: 3. *conclude*)
- Direct students to As You Read the Passage. Ask a volunteer to read the instructions aloud and have students complete the activity.
- After students finish reading the passage, direct them to After You Read the Passage. Have them complete the activity.

Student page 235

▶ Discuss with a Partner

Answers

1. D, paragraph 3
2. A, paragraphs 3 & 4
3. C, paragraphs 4 & 5
4. B, paragraph 8

- Have pairs of students share their answers to the questions about the passage and explain their thinking to each other and then to the class.
- Direct students to Discuss with a Partner and have them answer the questions and discuss their answers.
- Regroup as a class and have students share their answers with the class.

Reteach

If students are having difficulty drawing conclusions and making inferences, have them do the following activity.

- Draw a blank conclusion chart on the board.
- Write *desert, ocean, rain forest,* and *woods* beside it.
- Tell students you will give them clues and they will draw a conclusion about where the story takes place.
- Write *tall trees, parrots,* and *very rainy* in the chart. Under Conclusion, write *The story takes place in the _____.* (rain forest)
- Invite students to generate details about the other places and repeat the activity.

Objective

To use the skills and tools learned in Steps 1 and 2 and the tools learned in the beginning of Step 3 to answer prediction questions independently.

Student page 236

> ### Review the Skill

Students review how to make predictions.

- Remind students that a prediction is what you think will happen, based on the evidence and clues in a passage.
- Give examples and ask students to make predictions. Example: *What might happen at the beach if you forget to put on sunscreen?*

Check Back

Have students review signal words on page 152.

> ### Apply What You've Learned

Have students review and use tools that will help them identify and answer questions about making predictions.

- Direct students to Before You Read the Passage and ask a volunteer to read the instructions aloud. Have students complete the activity. (signal words in questions: 1. *prediction* 2. *clue* 3. *evidence* 4. *probably happened*)
- Direct students to As You Read the Passage and ask a volunteer to read the instructions aloud. Have students complete the activity.
- After students finish reading the passage, direct them to After You Read the Passage. Have them complete the activity.

Student page 238

> ### Discuss with a Partner

- Pair students and invite them to share their answers to the questions about the passage and explain their thinking to each other and then to the class.
- Direct students to the box at the bottom of the page and have them answer the questions and discuss their answers.
- Regroup as a class and have students share their answers.

Answers

1. B, paragraph 5
2. D, paragraph 5
3. A, paragraph 7
4. C, paragraph 7

Reteach

If students are having difficulty, have them do the following activity.

- Ask a student to describe his or her favorite activity. (example: baseball)
- Say *If you saw a boy walking toward the park dressed in a baseball uniform, carrying a bat and a glove, what would you predict he is going to do?* (He's going to play baseball.)
- Ask *How do you know?* (uniform, bat, glove)
- Draw a predictions web on the board and fill in the answers.
- Say *So we used these clues to predict that he is going to play baseball.*
- Invite students to generate their own examples and repeat the exercise.

```
                    ┌─────────────────────────┐
                    │       Prediction        │
                    │ Ask What will happen next?│
                    │                         │
                    │ He is going to play baseball.│
                    └─────────────────────────┘
          ┌───────────────┼───────────────┐
┌──────────────┐  ┌──────────────┐  ┌──────────────┐
│     Clue     │  │     Clue     │  │     Clue     │
│ Ask What clues│  │ Ask What clues│  │ Ask What clues│
│ help predict what│ help predict what│ help predict what│
│ will happen? │  │ will happen? │  │ will happen? │
│              │  │              │  │              │
│   Wearing a  │  │ Carrying a bat│  │  Wearing a glove│
│baseball uniform│ │              │  │              │
└──────────────┘  └──────────────┘  └──────────────┘
```

Objective

To use the skills and tools learned in Steps 1 and 2 and the tools learned in the beginning of Step 3 to answer questions about summary independently.

Student page 239 ▶ **Review the Skill**

Students review how to identify examples of summarizing in a passage.

- Remind students that a summary explains the most important parts of a passage in fewer words, including all of the main ideas.
- Give examples and ask students to summarize. Tie in to a current event or activity at school or in the community, e.g., what happens during a fire drill, recent field trips, school safety.

Check Back

Have students review the strategy for identifying summary information on page 155.

Apply What You've Learned

Have students review and use tools that will help them identify and answer questions about summarizing.

- Direct students to Before You Read the Passage. Ask a volunteer to read the instructions aloud and have students complete the activity.
- Direct students to As You Read the Passage. Ask a volunteer to read the instructions aloud and have students complete the activity.
- After students finish reading the passage, direct them to After You Read the Passage. Have them complete the activity.

Student page 241 ▶ **Discuss with a Partner**

Answers
1. C
2. B
3. A

- Have pairs of students share their answers to the questions about the passage and explain their thinking to each other and then to the class.
- Direct students to Discuss with a Partner and have them answer the questions and discuss their answers.
- Regroup as a class and have students share their answers with the class.

Reteach

If students are having difficulty with summarizing, have them do the following activity.

- Ask *How do you help out around the house?*
- Draw a web on the board and fill in the circles with answers, e.g., *wash dishes, vacuum the floor, take out trash.*
- Say *So we could say that students in this class really help out around the house.*
- Write *Students in this class really help out around the house* in the center box of the web.
- Explain that the box in the center contains a summary of the class discussion. Rather than list every activity in the summary, only the most important idea is included.

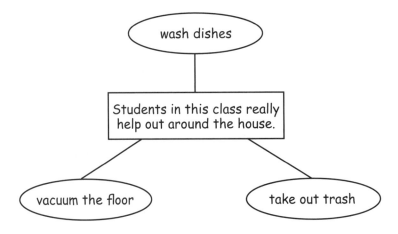

Answers

Arches National Park

1. A Incorrect. The passage does not indicate anything about the amount of water the animals need.
    B Incorrect. There is no indication in the passage about the animals scaring visitors.
    C **Correct. The description of the harsh conditions of the park leads to the inference that the animals there can live in those conditions.**
    D Incorrect. The passage does not indicate any preferences the animals may have.

2. A Incorrect. The statement *can* be proved.
    B Incorrect. The statement *can* be proved.
    C Incorrect. The statement *can* be proved.
    D **Correct. The statement *cannot* be proved, clearly expressing an opinion.**

3. A Incorrect. The passage does not suggest that people study the animals.
    B **Correct. The rocks are the reason people visit the park.**
    C Incorrect. The passage does not suggest that people bathe in the potholes.
    D Incorrect. The passage does not suggest that visitors are allowed to climb the mountains.

4. A Incorrect. The park's unique geologic formations will last for centuries, so the park will continue to interest people.
    B Incorrect. There is nothing in the passage that suggests that this might happen.
    C Incorrect. The passage does not provide any clues to suggest that this might occur.
    D **Correct. This is the most logical prediction to make based on the information in the passage.**

5. A Incorrect. The passage is informative, not entertaining.
    B Incorrect. The passage informs the reader about the park, not the state it's in.
    C **Correct. The passage includes positive, persuasive opinions about the park.**
    D Incorrect. The passage mentions arches but does not attempt to persuade the reader to like them.

6. A Incorrect. This answer includes details and not the most important parts of the passage.
    B Incorrect. This answer does not include the most important parts of the passage.
    C **Correct. This answer includes the most important parts of the passage and the main ideas.**
    D Incorrect. This answer includes details and not the most important parts of the passage.

Answers

The Bucket Game

1. A Incorrect. While Sean may be tired after playing, it is not the best word to describe him here.
   B Incorrect. Based on the details in the passage, Sean does not appear to be irritated.
   C **Correct. Sean says that he is very sorry at the end of the passage.**
   D Incorrect. The passage does not include details that suggest that Sean is worried.

2. A **Correct. All of the action takes place at Sean's house.**
   B Incorrect. The passage does not mention a park.
   C Incorrect. The passage mentions Sean's mother in a kitchen, but that is one part of the setting.
   D Incorrect. Some action takes place in the closet, but that is one part of the setting.

3. A Incorrect. Sean's mom started the roast *before* he searched for a bucket.
   B Incorrect. He searched for a bucket *after* Won called.
   C **Correct. Sean moved the plant *after* he had searched for and found a bucket.**
   D Incorrect. Sean read a magazine *before* he searched for a bucket.

4. A Incorrect. Sean's sister never speaks of Won, or of Sean's playing with Won.
   B Incorrect. The passage does not say whether Won said hello.
   C **Correct. Sean's sister was angry at him for ruining her science project.**
   D Incorrect. The sister became upset as a result of Sean's actions, not her mother's anger.

5. A Incorrect. There is no mention of water in Sean's room when his mother says this.
   B Incorrect. Sean has not dumped out any soil when his mother says this.
   C Incorrect. There is no mud in Sean's room when his mother says this.
   D **Correct. Sean's mother used this simile to indicate that she thought the room was not clean enough.**

6. A Incorrect. This answer is not how *pace* is used in the passage.
   B **Correct. A *rate of speed* best defines how *pace* is used in the passage.**
   C Incorrect. This answer is not how *pace* is used in the passage.
   D Incorrect. This answer is not how *pace* is used in the passage.

7. A **Correct. The story focuses on the consequences of Sean's shortcuts.**
   B Incorrect. There is no pattern of kindness in the passage.
   C Incorrect. It is true that Sean avoided hard work, but the story focuses more on the consequences of his shortcuts due to his laziness.
   D Incorrect. The passage ends before anyone forgives Sean for his actions.

The Block Party

8. A Incorrect. Based on the details in the passage, David does not appear to be worried.
   B **Correct. David helps his father, even when David is tired.**
   C Incorrect. There is nothing in the passage that suggests David is silly; just the opposite, he seems to be very serious and responsible.
   D Incorrect. When his father wakes David at nine o'clock, he is *a little confused*, but otherwise he understands everything that is going on.

9. A Incorrect. In the passage, David is not particularly quiet, and neither is Gina.
   B Incorrect. David does not say or do funny things in the passage, and Gina does not either.
   C **Correct. David shows he is responsible throughout the passage, while Gina avoids responsibility.**
   D Incorrect. The passage does not describe either David or Gina as being particularly happy.

10. A Incorrect. The prefix *dis-* can mean *not*. The meaning of "to not regard" is not the same as *understood*.
    B Incorrect. The meaning of "to not regard" is not the same as *confused*.
    C Incorrect. The meaning of "to not regard" is not the same as *respected*.
    D **Correct. The meaning of "to not regard" is the same as *ignored*.**

11. A   Incorrect. *Play with* is not a synonym; it means something completely different.
    B   Incorrect. *Look at* is not a synonym, it means something completely different.
    C   Incorrect. *Annoy* is not a synonym, it means to make angry or upset.
    D   **Correct. The words *assist* and *help* can have the same meaning.**

12. A   Incorrect. Gina never appears to love to work.
    B   **Correct. This continues the pattern of behavior described in the passage.**
    C   Incorrect. The party has not yet started, so it would not make sense for the net to be taken down.
    D   Incorrect. This has already happened, so it cannot happen next.

13. A   **Correct. This sums up what happens in the passage.**
    B   Incorrect. This is a small part of the passage and does not summarize what happens.
    C   Incorrect. This does not fully describe Gina's part in the passage.
    D   Incorrect. This does not sum up what happened in the passage.

The Indianapolis 500

14. A   Incorrect. This cannot be proved so it is an opinion.
    B   Incorrect. This statement cannot be proved, so it is an opinion.
    C   **Correct. This is stated in the passage and can be proved.**
    D   Incorrect. This is an opinion and cannot be proved.

15. A   Incorrect. There is nothing in the passage that suggests this.
    B   **Correct. The passage's details and facts show that the race is a very big event.**
    C   Incorrect. This may be true, but it is not the main idea of the passage.
    D   Incorrect. Although this is true, the passage does not mention it or imply it.

16. A   Incorrect. This section describes only what it's like to be at the race.
    B   Incorrect. The names of drivers are not mentioned in this section.
    C   Incorrect. This section mentions the first driver but no others.
    D   **Correct. This section discusses significant drivers, including the oldest driver ever to win, so information about the youngest driver would also be here.**

17. A   Incorrect. In 1925, the average speed was 101 miles per hour.
    B   Incorrect. In 1950, the average speed was 124 miles per hour.
    C   Incorrect. In 1975, the average speed was 149 miles per hour.
    D   **Correct. The year 2000 is the only one in the chart that shows an average speed of more than 150 miles per hour.**

18. A   Incorrect. While the passage informs the reader about the race, it does not try to persuade the reader to attend the race as an amusement park guide may do.
    B   **Correct. The passage provides information about the race and also contains opinions, which are both appropriate for a sports magazine.**
    C   Incorrect. The passage contains opinions and is therefore not suitable for an encyclopedia.
    D   Incorrect. While the passage is informative, it does not report on current events as a newspaper article does.

19. A   **Correct. Context clues say that cars speed, or go close to 200 miles per hour.**
    B   Incorrect. The context clues do not suggest that the cars inch.
    C   Incorrect. The context clues do not suggest that the cars stop.
    D   Incorrect. Context clues do not suggest that the cars park on the track.

20. A   Incorrect. The passage does not encourage the reader to become a driver in the race.
    B   **Correct. The passage informs the reader about the race.**
    C   Incorrect. The passage is informative, not entertaining.
    D   Incorrect. The passage makes no attempt to warn the reader about the race's dangers.

Student Skill Progress Chart

Use these charts to monitor student performance. The charts show the item numbers for each skill tested in the unit and step reviews. Circle the number for any question the student answers incorrectly. If the student requires additional instruction, use the Skills Instruction chart on the inside back cover to find the pages where each skill is taught.

Student Name: _____

Unit 1: Comprehension		Step 1		Step 2		Step 3	
		Unit 1 Review Questions	Step 1 Review Questions	Unit 1 Review Questions	Step 2 Review Questions	Unit 1 Review Questions	Step 3 Review Questions
1	Main idea and supporting details	1, 2	1	7	6	1, 5	15
2	Sequence	5, 6	3	4, 5	13	2	3
3	Compare and contrast	7, 8	6	1, 6	2	4	9
4	Cause and effect	3, 4	5	2, 3	14	3	4

Unit 2: Fiction and Nonfiction Skills		Step 1		Step 2		Step 3	
		Unit 2 Review Questions	Step 1 Review Questions	Unit 2 Review Questions	Step 2 Review Questions	Unit 2 Review Questions	Step 3 Review Questions
5	Character	2	7	7	4	4	1
6	Plot and setting	3	4	5	3	5	2
7	Theme	1	17	4	1	6	7
8	Literary elements	4	20	6	20	7	5
9	Structural elements	5	8	1	10	2	16
10	Visual information	6	14	3	9	3	17
11	Nonfiction writing	7	11	2	8	1	18

© Harcourt Achieve Inc. All rights reserved. This page may be photocopied for educational use within each purchasing institution.

© Harcourt Achieve Inc. All rights reserved. This page may be photocopied for educational use within each purchasing institution.

Unit 3: Vocabulary		Step 1		Step 2		Step 3	
		Unit 3 Review Questions	Step 1 Review Questions	Unit 3 Review Questions	Step 2 Review Questions	Unit 3 Review Questions	Step 3 Review Questions
12	Root words, prefixes, and suffixes	2	2	2	18	2	10
13	Synonyms and antonyms	1, 3	13	3, 4	15	3	11
14	Context clues	4	15	1	19	1	19
15	Multiple-meaning words	5	9	5	5	4	6

Unit 4: Critical Thinking		Step 1		Step 2		Step 3	
		Unit 4 Review Questions	Step 1 Review Questions	Unit 4 Review Questions	Step 2 Review Questions	Unit 4 Review Questions	Step 3 Review Questions
16	Author's purpose	4	10	1	17	5	20
17	Facts and opinions	1	16	4	11	2	14
18	Draw conclusions and make inferences	2, 6	18	3, 6	12	1, 3	8
19	Make predictions	3	19	5	16	4	12
20	Summarize	5	12	2	7	6	13

Comments:

_____

_____

_____

_____

_____

Skills and Items Correlation

Unit 1: Comprehension		Step 1		Step 2		Step 3	
		Unit 1 Review Questions	Step 1 Review Questions	Unit 1 Review Questions	Step 2 Review Questions	Unit 1 Review Questions	Step 3 Review Questions
1	Main idea and supporting details	1, 2	1	7	6	1, 5	15
2	Sequence	5, 6	3	4, 5	13	2	3
3	Compare and contrast	7, 8	6	1, 6	2	4	9
4	Cause and effect	3, 4	5	2, 3	14	3	4
Unit 2: Fiction and Nonfiction Skills		Unit 2 Review Questions	Step 1 Review Questions	Unit 2 Review Questions	Step 2 Review Questions	Unit 2 Review Questions	Step 3 Review Questions
5	Character	2	7	7	4	4	1
6	Plot and setting	3	4	5	3	5	2
7	Theme	1	17	4	1	6	7
8	Literary elements	4	20	6	20	7	5
9	Structural elements	5	8	1	10	2	16
10	Visual information	6	14	3	9	3	17
11	Nonfiction writing	7	11	2	8	1	18
Unit 3: Vocabulary		Unit 3 Review Questions	Step 1 Review Questions	Unit 3 Review Questions	Step 2 Review Questions	Unit 3 Review Questions	Step 3 Review Questions
12	Root words, prefixes, and suffixes	2	2	2	18	2	10
13	Synonyms and antonyms	1, 3	13	3, 4	15	3	11
14	Context clues	4	15	1	19	1	19
15	Multiple-meaning words	5	9	5	5	4	6
Unit 4: Critical Thinking		Unit 4 Review Questions	Step 1 Review Questions	Unit 4 Review Questions	Step 2 Review Questions	Unit 4 Review Questions	Step 3 Review Questions
16	Author's purpose	4	10	1	17	5	20
17	Facts and opinions	1	16	4	11	2	14
18	Draw conclusions and make inferences	2, 6	18	3, 6	12	1, 3	8
19	Make predictions	3	19	5	16	4	12
20	Summarize	5	12	2	7	6	13

© Harcourt Achieve Inc. All rights reserved. This page may be photocopied for educational use within each purchasing institution.